DATE DUE

Demco, Inc. 38-293

User-Friendly Schools for Latinos

A Model for All Immigrants

Robert Ricken
Michael Terc

Rowman & Littlefield Education
Lanham, Maryland • Toronto • Oxford
2006

Published in the United States of America
by Rowman & Littlefield Education
A Division of Rowman & Littlefield Publishers, Inc.
A wholly owned subsidary of The Rowman & Littlefield Publishing Group, Inc.
4501 Forbes Boulevard, Suite 200, Lanham, Maryland 20706
www.rowmaneducation.com

PO Box 317
Oxford
OX2 9RU, UK

British Library Cataloguing in Publication Information Available

Library of Congress Cataloging-in-Publication Data

Ricken, Robert.
   User-friendly schools for Latinos : a model for all immigrants / Robert Ricken,
Michael Terc.
      p.   cm.
   Includes index.
      ISBN 1–57886–308–2 (hardcover : alk. paper)—ISBN 1–57886–309–0 (pbk. :
   alk. paper)   1. Hispanic Americans—Education.   2. Minorities—Education—
   United States.   3. Multicultural education—United States.   4. Community and
   school—United States.   5. School year—Planning.   I. Terc, Michael, 1946–   II.
   Title.
   LC2669.R53   2006
   371.829′68073—dc22
                                                                            2005018471

♾ ™ The paper used in this publication meets the minimum requirements of
American National Standard for Information Sciences—Permanence of Paper for
Printed Library Materials, ANSI/NISO Z39.48–1992. Manufactured in the United
States of America.

To our families—for their love and support
To our students—our hope for the future
To our colleagues—who gave us the gift of
their professional practices

The inspiration for this book was provided by three outstanding teachers from the Freeport School District. Alma G. Rocha, Liliana Lynch, and Ana Maria Fruchtnis spent countless hours describing their district's efforts to meet the needs of Latino children and their parents. Their positive description of the program, staff, children, and parents of their school system made this text a labor of love. Each day they demonstrate a commitment to the teaching profession and to the community they so competently serve.

Contents

Introduction

At the start of this century, researchers informed educators that demographic studies indicated that students and families of Hispanic ancestry would become the largest minority group in U.S. schools. This book is intended to assist educators, school districts, and communities in learning and implementing a variety of techniques to reach out to our Hispanic residents. Visiting many New York City schools and more than 25 districts on Long Island, we began to collate many programs and activities that were in use to accomplish this task. At several conferences sponsored by the National Association of Secondary School Principals, we broadened our inquiries and involved principals from California, Texas, and Florida to discover what they were doing to make their Hispanic population feel they were a part of their school system.

When we completed our inquiries, we realized that these thoughtfully designed programs would be helpful to all immigrant populations. Additionally, we saw merit in using the ideas and activities when dealing with our Native American and African American children. Our own school district has a large Portuguese population, and although they are not classified as Hispanic, we also realized that most programs we were discussing would prove beneficial to our district's children and their families.

After determining which ideas are meaningful for their own Hispanic community, we hope our readers consider the ways each program could be adopted or adapted for any other of their minority populations.

It has been said that if you steal from one person it is plagiarism. If you steal from many, it is considered scholarship. Thus this work is a scholarly endeavor since we have networked with many educators, and we present here their collective ideas, activities, and programs.

CHAPTER 1

Responding to the Needs of Our Increasing Hispanic School Population

Deeds not words.

—Mother Teresa

In the determination of which foreign-language community to use as our model program, we decided to focus upon immigrants of Hispanic background. Futurists predict that no other ethnic minority will do more to change the demographics of the United States than will our Hispanic immigrants. Their numbers have surpassed the African American community, and they have become our nation's largest minority group for children in kindergarten through grade 12. Most experts predict this extraordinary growth will continue, and they project that in 2 decades one out of every four students in U.S. elementary schools will be from a Spanish-speaking family.

Administrators should note that Hispanic Americans are in no way a homogeneous community. They have emigrated from many countries and continents. Many people in the Northeast originally thought of Hispanics as being Puerto Ricans since they arrived in great numbers, particularly since the 1950s. In Florida Cuban Americans fled Castro in huge waves of immigration, and cities such as Miami presently have sizable Cuban populations. These relatively new citizens are making major inroads in the fields of business and politics. In the South and Southwest, Mexican Americans are changing the population statistics of large states such as Texas and California. Hispanic Americans have emigrated from North, Central, and South America, including Mexico, Guatemala, and Salvador, in addition to Cuba and Puerto Rico.

Staff members must remember that cultures and even dialects of Hispanic students and families are often quite different even though we statistically categorize them as Hispanic. It is easy to overlook these differences and to stereotype the entire community. In a recent graduate class in school administration, the professor reported that three of his students spoke Spanish as their native language. He admitted that his assumption was that they were all of Cuban or Puerto Rican heritage. When they reported on their school's bilingual program, they revealed they were from Mexico, Ecuador, and Africa. He admitted to having succumbed to a form of cultural typecasting.

In any study of the Hispanic community, teachers may in an unbiased manner learn of the many shared similarities, such as the Spanish language, certain values, and aspects of a common culture. In developing a program to reach out to children and parents of the Hispanic community, principals and teachers should reflect upon the following considerations of diverse cultures.

- Many children of Hispanic heritage might limit their conversations with authority figures. (Remember, teachers and particularly principals are often viewed as authority figures.)
- Contrary to the stereotype of their being highly emotional, many students and their parents will rarely display feelings of anger and frustration to school officials. They will be a "silent minority."
- As we will discuss in our epilogue, both our Asian students and their Hispanic classmates will often avoid eye contact when talking with authority figures.
- The children and their community are usually not driven by time, due dates, and punctuality.
- Cooperative learning might meet their needs since they are often not highly competitive.
- They are most comfortable with nonpressured interpersonal relationships. As we will note later, home visits and one-on-one private conversations are very effective in exploring their feelings about school, peers, and comfort levels.
- Praise, which holds them above their classmates, can make them extremely uncomfortable since some Hispanic cultures value cooperation, not competition.
- Machismo is a significant consideration, and males are usually the

privileged sex. One major challenge is improving opportunities for Hispanic girls and women without offending their families.

- There is also cultural pride in machismo since it refers to traits such as honor and dignity. Boys are taught to protect women, respect their family, and have affection for children. It is obviously not a trait that can be challenged without fully understanding these more positive concepts.
- As they must do with other immigrant foreign-born groups, educators must encourage activities that enhance an appreciation for the diversity of the Hispanic culture and promote the self-esteem of these students.

In our selection of the Spanish-speaking community, we recognize that a main thrust of this text is to value their participation in the school system. Parents are their child's first teacher. It is an indisputable fact that the involvement of parents enhances the learning opportunities for their children. Educational researchers unanimously agree that children do better academically and socially when their parents are encouraged to get involved with schools and educators. Educators must design strategies to encourage parental involvement.

In the remainder of this book, techniques to accomplish this goal will be explored and specific implementation methods will be described. The school district should consider these overall goals:

- The school staff must learn about the characteristics of the parents and families of their immigrant and minority students. Accomplishing this involves in-service courses and agreement that this should be one of the school's instructional priorities. Often there are staff members who do not necessarily see this as a job requirement. Techniques to address this resistance must also be implemented. Teachers should be reminded that when both parents are employed, it will be difficult for them to attend meetings scheduled during school hours. If families are on public assistance, the children may not be able to go on field trips, which require them to contribute money for admission and transportation.
- Communication with the family must go beyond what was the usual standard operating procedure. Many school letters should be

written in Spanish if staff is aware that parents can't read English. When in doubt, dual-language correspondence should be used. Discovering ways to inform parents about homework and assignments that are due should ultimately be viewed as a challenge and not a burden. In the next chapter, use of a community liaison will be recommended to reach out to parents in the comfort of their homes.

- We recognize that schools and their staff usually do an excellent job of securing feedback from their students. With parents who do not speak English, additional techniques must be used. Many districts have revised their exit-interview questionnaires and have written them in both languages. Other opportunities for these parents to offer their reactions to school activities and curricula should also be designed. The onus is on school personnel to develop the means to have parents and teachers work as a team. This obviously requires nurturing mutual respect.

- Some schools are selecting one foreign language in the elementary school to be taught to all students from kindergarten through grade 5. In schools with a large Spanish-speaking population, a great deal of mutual respect can be gained in addition to improved language skills. There is the additional opportunity to teach an appreciation of the culture of our non-English-speaking children.

- Creating ways these parents can help their children at home is another of the staff's responsibilities. We will be recommending learning activities designed for not only parents and family members but babysitters as well. Often, employed parents are forced to leave their children with non-English-speaking adults when they are at work. Offering these people learning materials will help the child to perform tasks similar to those he or she will be doing in school.

- Educators should become aware of the stress that children and families are experiencing in attempting to survive in a new land. Some parents are facing poverty, divorce, and coping with new traditions and even a different system of government. As we will discuss in our month-to-month activities, school-initiated partnerships with the community's service clubs, social organizations, church leaders, and city agencies are necessary. *Caring* is an action word!

- Although administrators are primarily educational ombudsmen for children, offering learning experiences for their parents is compatible with our adult-education goals. Courses in the school can include a full range of subjects, including English, computers, and arts and crafts, as well as augmenting parenting skills and gaining a high school equivalency diploma. Sometimes the availability of the library and bilingual materials will benefit parents in their quest to become true partners in the education of their children. Many schools also include a course that offers information on how to become a U.S. citizen.
- School staff should attempt to have Spanish-speaking parents provide learning activities to their children even if it's in their native language. Teacher-designed worksheets can be sent to homes or these skill-development activities could be taught at parenting workshops. These will be demonstrated in the techniques described for outreach teachers and community liaisons.

A priority in our goal to involve parents is the establishment of a school-community position. Many staff members perform the duties of this task under a variety of job descriptions and professional titles. Optimally, districts might wish to hire a school social worker to perform these tasks, but it has been found that adding a full-time certified member to the staff often becomes a roadblock to budget-minded school board members. It should be noted that people holding liaison positions in many school systems are simply members of the community who are trained by teachers and administrators to perform the tasks listed in the job description. Budgetary considerations should not be allowed to eliminate this needed service. Some districts have a resident in the community work at an hourly rate of pay for a few hours a day to perform these urgent duties. Many school districts have employed people for 4 hours a day, at an annual salary of less than $10,000 a year. These hours can be made flexible to allow the community employee to visit homes during the evening hours.

We have surveyed many school districts to elicit their job descriptions for the position of school-community liaison. They have a host of expectations for the position. There is no such thing as a typical job description. We have seen written job expectations for this position that ranged from describing duties of a completely uncertified worker to those of an assistant superintendent of schools. One such job description was for an administratively certified professional whose title was community-relations liaison, special-projects coordinator, and whose tasks included the following:

I.   Community liaison
    A. Coordinate all activities of the community coalition.
    B. Serve on the following community-related committees:
        1. community center advisory board
        2. community coalition
        3. youth council adult board
        4. community fund
    C. Serve as coordinator for reporting bias incidents occurring in the school and community.
II.   Adult-education coordinator
    A. Plan courses for the adult-education program.
    B. Develop adult programs for our foreign-born parents.
    C. Ensure that adult-education brochures are written in Spanish as well as English.
    D. Network with adjoining districts to discover additional programs for our indigenous and Spanish-speaking parents.
III. Director of bilingual center
    A. Develop Welcome Wagon package.
    B. Improve and refine bilingual adult parenting programs.
    C. Work cooperatively with community churches.
    D. Assist in organizing programs for the financially needy.
    E. Improve course for gaining U.S. citizenship.
    F. Continue the development of vocational-skills courses.
    G. Continue outreach activities with our parent-community committee.
    H. Explore the increase of school programs in the homes, churches, and social clubs of the Spanish-speaking community.
IV.   District schools liaison
    A. Develop a format to ensure every school is aware of the programs.
    B. Make at least one faculty presentation in each building annually.

   C. Provide Spanish-speaking people for parent-teacher confer-
      ences.
   D. Ensure inclusion of our immigrant community in each school's
      international day, art fairs, career days, and parent-teacher
      organizations.
   E. Encourage materials to be written in Spanish when mailed to
      our non-English-speaking parents.
   F. Conduct an annual exhibit in a different school to showcase
      the culture of our non-English-speaking parents.
V. Other
   A. Serve as liaison to all community organizations to encourage
      the inclusion of our foreign-born parents.
   B. Lead an annual board of education presentation on our pro-
      gram.
   C. Work with the superintendent on additional special projects.
   D. Involve village real estate businesses in annual demographic
      projections.

Some of these job expectations will be more fully explored in the
following chapter, but the brief discussion of those that follow will
allow administrators and teachers to understand the challenges they
will be confronting. No matter how many of the job descriptions we
reviewed, the tasks entrusted to the community-relations person were
quite similar. As with most jobs in education, the duties and job expectations far exceed the written job description.

Job expectations for the school-community liaison include the following:

- Identify newly arrived non-English-speaking families as soon as
  they move into the community.
- Develop and share a list of useful services that are offered in the
  district.
- Assist in the development of plans to help children learn English.
- Assist the parents with information about children's services and
  family assistance available from the school, village, or city.
- Provide educational materials to parents, especially for their
  preschool-age children.

- Develop collegial relationships with other community agencies such as service organizations, social clubs, religious institutions, and city social service employees.
- Meet regularly with school principals and the parent-teacher association (PTA).
- Develop social activities and assist the immigrant population to display artifacts of their culture. Offer their performing groups or artists the opportunity to showcase their talent in the school and community.
- Help to involve them in social activities such as the Scouts, Little League sports, and the PTA.
- Be an advocate for the parents to participate in adult-education courses.
- Involve parents in school activities such as career days, multicultural events, and cultural arts activities.
- Educate them about parental responsibilities and how to be partners in the education of their children.
- Assist with the translation of documents from civil and school authorities.
- Host frequent meetings with parents to discover their concerns and to implement the agenda of the school system.
- Become an advocate for non-English-speaking parents to inform community and school officials about their needs.
- Attempt to use the talents of members of your community to serve as role models for children and to enable staff members to use their areas of expertise.
- Become an active participant in Hispanic organizations that are advocates for our Spanish students and parents and that offer specialized services for their families.
- Serve as a translator in school-parent conferences to ensure that there is effective dual communication.
- Develop study- and homework-assistance classes in the school and in the homes of our foreign-language students.
- Establish a hotline to be used by students and parents whenever they have questions about the school or community.
- Network with other school districts and advocacy groups to remain

on the cutting edge of developing activities and to assist school officials with the implementation of new programs.

- Meet regularly with church officials to learn about families with unique or financial needs.
- Help the school develop a club advocating cultural diversity or an antibullying program.
- Work with school administrators to develop food, holiday toy, and clothing drives to earn field trip funds for the needy.
- Ensure that the school and community adhere to confidentiality laws in the operation of social service offerings such as the school district's required free and reduced-fee lunch program.

The commonality of the needs of the limited-English-speaking community has been described and documented. The activities that school administrators should implement have been listed and will be fully developed in the following chapters. Although we recommended a key role for a community-liaison employee, no such position may exist in your school district. As with everything else, the ultimate responsibility falls on the shoulders of the school principal.

The following poetically describes the administrator's recommended mode of operation:

"Love Me When I'm Most Unlovable!"

You spoke to me of love
I doubted you.
You spoke to me of caring
I doubted you.
You spoke to me of my self-worth
I doubted you.
You came to visit me in the hospital
I believed everything you said.

—Robert Ricken

It is clear that the school administrator must have a bias for action when addressing the needs of students and their foreign-born parents. The challenge is to mobilize the staff to view these as exciting opportunities, not as unwanted, additional responsibilities. Future chapters provide specific ideas and a set of implementation strategies.

CHAPTER 2

Proactive Efforts of the School and Community

To be prepared is half the victory.

—Miguel Cervantes

Any program to assist children and families of limited English proficiency should begin long before a child enters the school system. Most districts and states require children to begin their formal education in kindergarten. Some boards of education make policy decisions that enable youngsters to attend prekindergarten (pre-K) classes. Obviously, early formal instruction is advantageous to children who speak limited English and to those whose parents are foreign born. This recommendation is without any reservation. We do, however, recognize that many communities simply will not support additional expenditures, no matter how much research supports the benefits.

The superintendent should designate a person to represent the school system in its relations with the local government, service clubs, religious institutions, and other community-wide enterprises. We advocate a preference for a community liaison to coordinate the activities between all segments of the community and the families of children who are not fluent in English. The most critical element of any assistance initiative is to involve these parents early and often.

There have been several examples of U.S.-born Hispanic children who speak little or no English when they enter the school system, because they have been served by Spanish-speaking babysitters throughout their childhood. It is essential to reach out to these homes and assist the home-care provider with activities that will enhance the children's ability to speak English. Something as simple as worksheets listing items around the home that are written in both English and

Spanish can make for a good start. These are similar to many of the learning materials we will recommend for students in kindergarten and first grade. For an example see table 2.1.

Anyone can add to the list. It reminds the home-care providers that they can also help the children to learn English words while they attend to the business of monitoring their behavior and activities. One school-community representative has a wide range of worksheets that can be used when children go to stores, the playground, or the local park or when they are at home.

Working with the local political establishment also enhances the preschool children's learning activities. Village and city officials often sponsor poster contests for children. The topics include automotive safety, antidrug messages, holiday greetings, and the appreciation of foreign cultures. They afford children many learning opportunities and also develop latent skills.

Local charity drives can also involve our pre-K children. By their participation, they learn the social value of giving to poorer members of the community. Activities for months such as November and December often include school-sponsored food drives for the needy families in the community.

A special partnership should be fostered with organizations such as Welcome Wagon. When new residents move into a community, they generally receive a basket of discount coupons to local stores and many other items. Real estate agents are instrumental in providing the names and addresses of new residents for this purpose. Along with the gifts, the school-community representative should ensure that the school

Table 2.1   English and Spanish Words for Everyday Items

English	Spanish
house	casa
door	puerta
table	mesa
chair	silla
spoon	cuchao
fork	tenedor
bed	cama
desk	escritorio

adds its message and material to the basket. Minimally, a welcoming letter from the school superintendent or the president of the school board urging that the new residents become partners in the education of their children should be included. Many districts go beyond this formality and send home an invitation to tour the local school, a promise of a visit from a school-community official, and some ideas for parents to use at home to enhance their child's education. This type of proactive behavior is evidence of a caring school administration that doesn't simply pay lip service to community and parent involvement in school affairs.

A cooperative relationship with local religious establishments is another action high on any priority list. In the case of the Hispanic community, one would consider the Catholic Church a partner in these activities. All other churches, mosques, and synagogues should be members of the school's coalition to help these children. Religious officials are a wonderful resource in that they often have intimate knowledge of the children and the status of their families. Many schools will contact local priests, ministers, and rabbis to ascertain which families need help during the holiday seasons and throughout the year. In one school district, a principal noted that children were throwing around pennies when they received them as change for the cost of their lunch. He set up a jar in the cafeteria with a sign, "Change to Help Needy Families." Not only did the children donate their pennies, but often dimes and quarters were added. It brought meaning to the caring words on the loudspeaker exhorting students and faculty to help the needy throughout the year.

Clothing and toy drives are also popular activities. Many schools work with the U.S. Marine Corps and their Toys for Tots campaign. A close relationship with church officials enhances the opportunity to get the donations to the neediest families. It might be uncomfortable or embarrassing for a child to receive a gift of toys, clothing, or food from a classmate. Picking up these items at the church or having them given to parents by religious officials is seemingly more appropriate and minimizes any social stigma.

Some local churches have food pantries that are stocked with the aid of the entire community. School organizations such as the student council, athletic teams, key clubs, PTAs, faculty sunshine committees, and honor societies often are major contributors to this wonderful community service. This is an interfaith effort as well as a multiethnic charitable cause.

We have used the term *service organizations* and perhaps it needs a more specific definition. Associations such as Kiwanis, Elks, Rotary, chambers of commerce, Lions, and Knights of Columbus are active in most school communities. These clubs are composed of many adult men and women whose sole purpose is to offer help to members of the community and to promote the objectives of their organization. Schools should assign an administrator, a teacher, or a liaison to each of these worthy groups. As business owners, they often want to give back to the community and to the schools in appreciation for the residents who patronize their businesses and use their services. A principal has reported that a local service organization has for more than a decade donated funds to our foreign-born children who needed money for field trips and other school expenses. They also send a boy and girl to a 2-week summer camp to help enhance their academic or athletic skills.

Many religious institutions fund their own private schools within the confines of a school district. These church-related schools often have full-time day care services and nursery schools. Public schools that have an adversarial relationship with private or parochial schools often lose valuable opportunities to help the non-English-speaking community. One principle to remember is that these are all our children, and they usually play together after school is over. We strongly recommend that the school-community representative work in partnership with all schools in the boundaries of the district. Sharing ideas with the owners of private nursery schools and parochial schools may help students who might someday attend the public school.

A cooperative relationship gives credence to the school's objectives to educate both students and parents with limited English proficiency. Parents of children attending private schools may need the district's adult-education services. Welcoming them into our public schools increases their knowledge about various courses and activities offered to their children. Many foreign-born parents come from countries that have predominately church-operated schools. Other small villages in Hispanic countries support only church-run schools. Parents may even feel they are not doing right by their children if they send them to a public school. Local school systems may have to expose parents to the functions and mission of U.S. education.

Involvement in the community assists educators in celebrating our differences. Although public school teachers do not teach religion, they are encouraged to talk about religious holidays and customs. Private school children should be invited to participate in international days, multiethnic dinners, book fairs, and poster contests that celebrate diversity. One inclusive activity is to create an international cookbook that involves every segment of the town. Income from this venture can be used to support services for the less fortunate members of the community.

Even senior citizen organizations should be part of the community coalition to welcome foreign-born families. At times, the aged have to be reminded that, unless we're Native Americans, we were all once immigrants. They often become a resource for the schools by discussing their own immigration stories. Some relate interesting tales about how they came to America to escape persecution in their original homeland. Many communities have begun making audio and video recordings of these experiences to ensure their stories will be remembered years after they're gone. One principal reported that when the senior citizens in his district began to get involved in this type of project, much of their resentment of the newly arrived foreign-born residents ended.

Some districts invite senior citizen organizations to their multicultural celebrations and report that they now participate, tell their own experiences, and often bring samples of their favorite ethnic food. When the students perform ethnic dances and sing the songs of the country from which they emigrated, the older residents enjoy the programs. Since many seniors have problems with transportation, districts often send their multicultural performers to showcase their talents in the senior citizen's meeting halls. In one district, some of the seniors have become pen pals with these students.

Little League organizations and Police Boys and Girls Clubs have joined in this inclusion effort. Baseball leagues offer a great opportunity to have children play together and learn English. Many Hispanic youngsters have excellent soccer skills in addition to experience in baseball.

Some coaches are very cooperative and adhere to the community-liaison's request to give out a brief vocabulary list of sports items. For an example, see table 2.2.

Coaches have reported that when children play as a team, race and ethnicity are generally nonissues. Most coaches live in the community, and that further contributes to the Hispanic children's acceptance by local community families. These adult volunteers have observed that after the games children originally went home with friends from their own culture. As time went by, there was a noticeable increase in inter-ethnic friendships. The leaders felt that there were few language barriers when the children were playing sports. If anything, it simply disappeared on the athletic field. Coaches also used Hispanic professional athletes as role models for their teams since there are so many involved in major league baseball. The present era has seen a proliferation of Hispanic athletic heroes, from Pele in soccer to Roberto Clemente in baseball. It is not difficult to point to these men as great athletes as well as humanitarians. It is an additional source of pride for our Hispanic youth.

The PTA, under proper leadership, can become a vital organization in the principal's mission to assist in the integration of Hispanics into the community and school. In a district where there was a large influx of Hispanic families, the PTA added the following activities to its regularly scheduled meetings.

- They inaugurated an annual Welcome to New Residents Program. The school's goals were shared as were the PTA's programs, services, and offerings.
- They held an international day and invited all residents to set up tables and display artifacts of their culture.

Table 2.2   English and Spanish Words for Baseball Terms

English	Spanish
baseball	beisbol
ball	pelota
bat	bate
coach	entrenador
glove	guante
hat	sombrero

- They hosted an international dinner in which everyone in attendance was able to sample a variety of ethnic foods.
- They joined with the school's student council to host an August tour of the school and had school administrators conduct a question-and-answer session. Spanish-speaking interpreters were available throughout the day.
- They established a bilingual parent committee to make sure these parents' concerns were communicated at meetings.
- They made a commitment to have interpreters present at all future meetings.
- They made a commitment to work with local political officials to organize multicultural events.

When we recommend the involvement of the entire community, we do not exclude small business establishments in the town, the local library, and financial institutions. The neighborhood banks receive television sets and videotape players from the school's audio-visual department. Videotapes of previous multicultural events are played for the enjoyment of the bank's customers and poster displays advertise the dates for upcoming community events. Smaller business establishments are equally happy to display posters and videos in their windows to demonstrate their community spirit.

One principal informed us of an extremely inventive idea to communicate with all segments of his school and community. He has amassed a list of every organization in town, business establishments, parent leaders, local service organization presidents, senior citizen clubs, and many other respected members of the school district. He refers to them as his "key communicators." His secretary has developed a telephone message chain that the principal activates whenever there are important upcoming events. In this way, he is able to inform all segments of the community about international days, art festivals, and music-of-all-nations concerts. Every representative on the list is asked to inform his own constituency and call the next person or organization listed. This is the administrator's way to make certain everyone is invited and no person or group feels left out or alienated.

When the faculty and members of school organizations collectively address the needs of foreign-born parents and their children, an energy is unleashed that is bound to have positive impact. Good things begin to happen. The recognition of common goals creates a renewed sensitivity toward the plight of immigrants. Most districts have incorporated these values into the school's mission statement and codes of conduct. State education departments have required districts to update their board-of-education policy statements to include items such as civility, citizenship, and character education. These obviously have ramifications for our growing immigrant population.

Bullying and ethnic slurs are offenses addressed in most codes of conduct, and they are deemed major transgressions by principals and staff members. Persecuting a classmate because of his race, religion, or heritage is a major disciplinary infraction. Name-calling was not always taken seriously by staff members. Often there was a "kids will be kids" attitude and a disregard for the pain caused by the hostile terms. In contemporary schools, these derogatory expressions are no longer tolerated. Across the nation civility, citizenship, and good character are deemed important values for families, schools, and communities. In many districts, awards for good character are beginning to rival those for academic achievement.

In most school board handbooks, character education is now stressed and is often reflected in board-of-education policy documents. This educational emphasis should include the instruction of students on the principles of

- honesty
- tolerance
- personal responsibility
- respect for others
- observance of rules and laws
- courtesy
- appreciation of the religions and cultures of all Americans

The recognition of these principles and challenges has become a part of most schools' action agenda. They are no longer themes to be stated without feeling or implementation strategies. Schools and communities are being asked to live by the values expressed in the Bill of Rights. Hate is a means to exclude others, whereas the valuing of our cultural differences is why the United States is inclusive and unique among nations.

The Anti-Defamation League (ADL) has produced a document of 101 ideas for building a prejudice-free zone in schools, homes, and communities. These items serve as an excellent all-inclusive review of the action strategies recommended for principals, school districts, and their community liaisons.

PREJUDICE: 101 WAYS YOU CAN BEAT IT!

In Your Home

1. Know your roots and share your pride in your heritage with others.
2. Celebrate holidays with extended family. Use such opportunities to encourage storytelling and share personal experiences across generations.
3. Invite friends from backgrounds different from your own to experience the joy of your traditions and customs.
4. Be mindful of your language; avoid stereotypical remarks and challenge those made by others.
5. Speak out against jokes and slurs that target people or groups. Silence sends a message that you are in agreement. It is not enough to refuse to laugh.
6. Be knowledgeable; provide as much accurate information as possible to reject harmful myths and stereotypes. Discuss as a family the impact of prejudicial attitudes and behavior.
7. Plan family outings to diverse neighborhoods in and around your community and visit local museums, galleries, and exhibits that celebrate art forms of different cultures.
8. Visit important landmarks in your area associated with the struggle for human and civil rights such as museums, public libraries, and historical sites.
9. Research your family tree and trace your family's involvement in the struggle for civil and human rights or the immigration experience. Identify personal heroes and positive role models.
10. Read and encourage your children to read books that promote understanding of different cultures as well as those that are written by authors of diverse backgrounds.

In Your School

11. Recite the A World of Difference Institute pledge, or a similar pledge against prejudice created by your student body, at a school-wide assembly.
12. Display a poster-size version of the pledge in a prominent area of your school and encourage people to sign it.
13. Establish a Diversity Club that serves as an umbrella organization to promote harmony and respect for differences. Reach out to sports teams, drama clubs, and language clubs for ideas and involvement. If your school already has a Diversity Club, hold a membership drive.
14. Initiate classroom discussions of terms such as anti-Semitism, racism, sexism, homophobia, and bias. Then compose a list of definitions and post it in a prominent place.
15. Invite a motivational speaker who is a recognized civil or human rights leader to address an all-school assembly. Videotape the speech and publish an interview with the speaker in the school and local newspapers.
16. Organize an essay contest whose theme is either a personal experience with prejudice or a success story in the fight against it. Suggest that the winning entries be published in your school newspaper, featured in your town newspaper, highlighted on a local cable program, or sent to the ADL office.
17. Create an anti-prejudice slogan for your school that could be printed as a bumper sticker and sold in the wider community to raise funds for these efforts.
18. Hold a "Rock Against Racism" or a concert, dance-a-thon, bike-a-thon, car wash, or battle-of-the-bands and donate the proceeds from ticket sales to underwrite diversity training and other programs for the school.
19. Form a student-faculty committee to write "Rules of Respect" for your school and display the finished set of rules in every classroom.
20. Invite your district attorney, police chief, or a representative from the attorney general's office to speak to your school about civil rights, hate crimes, and other legal aspects of the fight against prejudice.
21. Designate a wall space on or near school grounds where graffiti with a harmonious and unifying message can be written, drawn, or painted.
22. Publish a newsletter specifically devoted to promoting respect for diversity and publicizing multicultural events. Try to have your local newspaper or community Internet home page do the same.
23. Encourage representation of all students on every school board, committee, group, publication, and team.

24. Write an original song/chant/rap that celebrates your school's diversity and perform it at school rallies and other events.

25. Create a flag or poster that symbolizes your school's ideal of diversity, and display it at games, assemblies, and other school events.

26. Hold a T-shirt contest to come up with a logo or slogan like "I Don't Put Up With Put-Downs." The winning T-shirt design could be printed and sold at your school bookstore or in local shops, at community events or sports competitions.

27. Create a calendar with all the holidays and important civil rights dates represented in your school community.

28. Participate in a poster campaign such as ADL's "You Can't Turn Your Face Away From Hate" that encourages people to intervene when confronted with instances of prejudice.

29. Create an orientation program that addresses the needs of students of all backgrounds so that they feel welcome when joining the student body.

30. Initiate a pin drive in which students look for pins with positive slogans and tack them onto a designated bulletin board in the student lounge or other central gathering area.

31. Poll your teachers about their ethnic/cultural backgrounds and experiences and their experiences with prejudice. Ask each to write a short paragraph on the subject that can be compiled along with photos in a teacher "mug book."

32. Produce a "Proud Out Loud" video comprised of interviews with students and their grandparents about their ethnic heritage and why they are proud of it.

33. Host a Poetry Slam in which students read aloud original poems/raps that break down stereotypes and promote respect for diversity. Invite participants to present their work to PTA meetings, chamber of commerce events, and other community groups.

34. Research pro-diversity Web sites. Then build a Web page for your school and link it to others on the Internet.

35. Contact ADL about monitoring hate activities on the Internet.

36. Create a student-run Speakers Bureau where students of different backgrounds speak about their heritage. Identify local community leaders, civil rights [leaders], veterans, Holocaust survivors, and others to partner with students in this effort.

37. Devise a skit contest with themes that promote diversity.

38. Turn a school assembly into a game show for students of all grades called "Cultural Pursuit." Ask teachers to develop questions covering

every discipline and hold "culture bees" in their classrooms to determine assembly contestants.

39. Devote time in art classes to designing a Diversity Quilt with each patch
representing a student's individual heritage. Have all classes combine
their patchwork squares to form a school quilt for display in the community.

40. Organize a No-Ethnic-Humor Open-Mike Nite featuring stand-up com-
edy by students.

41. Meet with food services at your school to discuss the possibility of featuring ethnic cuisines on a regular basis. Consult with local restaurants
and community groups to participate in the program.

42. Request that a student-faculty committee establish an annual A World of
Difference Institute Day when regular classes are suspended and community members and leaders are invited to speak on and explore diversity with students. Consult with ADL to plan this program.

43. Construct a multimedia display that examines how today's media perpet-
uates stereotypes. Consider current films, television sitcoms, music and
advertising campaigns, in addition to newspapers, magazines, and
books.

44. Research peace negotiations going on around the world regarding ethnic
or racial conflict. Then stage a Mock Summit in which students take on
the roles of international leaders and try to resolve these crises.

45. Look for examples of youth who have struggled to overcome oppression
throughout history and create an original dramatic performance based
on their experiences.

46. Sponsor a "Dance for Diversity" dance-a-thon and approach a local
radio station about broadcasting live from your event. The station could
also run student-written public service announcements leading up to and
following the event.

47. Establish a school exchange that matches students from different schools
to bring youth of differing backgrounds closer together.

48. Start an annual multicultural film festival at your school. Invite community groups and local theaters to be cosponsors.

49. Recreate the Ellis Island Immigration Station for a school-wide event.
Involve teachers from all disciplines to create period costumes and sce-
nery and to prepare traditional foods. Issue passports to all students
attending and lead "new immigrants" through the interview process.

50. Collect samples of popular teen magazines and comic books from
around the world. Ask your librarian to set aside a special corner for
them in the periodical room.

51. Research children's books representing the experiences of different ethnic groups. Then initiate a reading program with a local bookstore or library that features these books.
52. Survey local card and gift shops for product lines geared to diverse groups. Write to greeting card companies and local merchants to advocate for expanding the diversity of selections. Coordinate a contest to create a line of cards/note paper that promotes respect for diversity.
53. Approach the guidance office about hosting a career workshop led by professionals who can discuss diversity in their respective fields.
54. Ask your school to host an Internship Fair for groups such as ADL and other civic organizations that hire student interns.
55. Advocate for the production of school plays that are sensitive to multiculturalism and incorporate a variety of roles and perspectives representing a diverse cast, audience, and story.
56. Ensure that musical selections of school bands and choruses are culturally diverse.
57. Speak to each of your teachers about posting a list somewhere in the classroom of famous pioneers/leaders in their field with a special focus on diversity.
58. Collect famous speeches about civil rights. Put them together in a binder or in a video collection and make it available to your whole school community.
59. Research civil unrest in this country from rebellions during slavery to Chicago in the 1960s to Los Angeles in the 1990s.
60. Survey the colleges in your area about diversity and affinity clubs at their schools. Invite a panel of representatives to speak to the senior class about "Prejudice on the College Campus: What To Look For—What To Do."

In Your Work Place

61. Make respect for diversity a core value in your company and articulate it as such in the company's handbook/employee manual.
62. Provide ongoing awareness programs about the value of human diversity for all employees in the organization.
63. Take advantage of diversity consultants and training programs such as the A World of Difference Institute's A Workplace of Difference to assist you with ongoing education.
64. Incorporate diversity as a business goal. Secure a high degree of commitment from all employees.

65. Become aware and respectful of individual work styles.
66. Create an environment conducive to the exploration of diversity.
67. Learn about coworkers' backgrounds and share your own. Ask questions that invite explanation and answer with the same.
68. Create a display area where employees can post notices of events and activities happening in their communities.
69. Publish and distribute to all staff a list of ethnic and/or religious holidays and the meaning of the customs associated with celebrating them.
70. Sponsor a lunchtime "brown-bag" series that features speakers on diversity topics.
71. Sponsor a mentoring program and reach out to students in local high schools and colleges.
72. Provide opportunities to attend local cultural events and exhibits.
73. Participate as a sponsor in community events that support the health and welfare of society.

In Your House of Worship

74. Urge your leaders to use the pulpit to condemn all forms of bigotry.
75. Encourage friends of other faiths to visit your religious services and share your religious knowledge with them.
76. Invite clergy representing religions different from your own to participate in services and deliver the sermon.
77. Host a tour for elected and appointed city/town officials to learn more about your religion and the programs and activities your religious community offers.
78. Ensure that all faiths are represented accurately in existing library materials and religious school curricula.
79. Reach out to diverse religious communities to co-sponsor festivals and holiday observances, such as ADL's Interfaith Seders, that highlight and celebrate our common humanity.
80. Be respectful of everyone who attends your religious services whether they are members of or visitors to your congregation.
81. Turn one bulletin board into a display space where newspaper/magazine clippings depicting current events related to anti-Semitism and other forms of religious persecution or human rights violations can be posted for all to read.
82. Organize an interfaith retreat for young people to increase understanding of each other's beliefs and build lasting friendships.
83. Plan an interfaith youth group trip to the U.S. Holocaust Memorial

Museum in Washington, DC. Raise funds to cover travel expenses with a community bake sale, car wash, service auction, or other activity.

In Your Community

84. Establish a Human Rights Commission and a Community Watch Group in your city/town.
85. Organize a local multicultural committee that serves as an umbrella organization for groups that raise awareness about prejudice and provide support for cultural events, holiday programs, or community efforts that promote intergroup harmony.
86. Volunteer to serve on one of these organizations' committees and work to support their initiatives.
87. Petition government officials to issue a proclamation making your city/ town a prejudice-free zone.
88. Plan a community-wide "Walk/Run Against Hate" in which sponsored participants would donate all monies pledged to an anti-bias or other human rights organization.
89. Become aware of your city/town's demographics and compare it to others around the state to better understand the diversity in your community.
90. Hold a city-wide Human Rights Day. Contact representatives of the Reebok Human Rights Board, Amnesty International, ADL, and other human rights organizations to participate.
91. Build a community float that promotes understanding and respect for the diversity of your community and march in local and state parades.
92. Contact parade officials to make sure that groups of all different backgrounds are invited to march.
93. Suggest to your local newspaper that it devote a corner of the editorial page each month to at least one opinion piece relating to anti-prejudice and pro-diversity themes.
94. Meet with school and community librarians and local bookstores to discuss ways to highlight literature that is representative of all culture.
95. Compile a citizen's directory of the businesses and community organizations that exist to support diverse groups in the community.
96. Research your town/community's involvement in struggles for civil and human rights throughout history, e.g., abolition, the civil rights movement, etc., and create an exhibit for the local library/town hall.
97. Discuss alternative accessibility routes such as ramps, stairs, and eleva-

tors in your community and invite speakers into your school and community groups to talk about such initiatives.

98. Make sure your public facilities accommodate the needs of all residents.

99. Collect traditional family recipes from local residents for a community
cookbook. Solicit ads to support the cost of reproducing and distributing
the book as part of a Welcome Wagon program for new residents.

100. Organize a city-wide "Hoops for Harmony" basketball tournament with
proceeds from ticket sales going to a local non-profit organization that
promotes awareness of and respect for diversity.

101. Hold a "Paint-Out Day" to eliminate graffiti that promotes bigotry, culminating with a potluck supper. (Anti-Defamation League, 2005)

CHAPTER 3

July: Establishing the Direction of Reaching-Out Activities for the School Year

Democracy means not "I am as good as you are," but "you are as good as I am."

—Theodore Parker

Every school year brings challenges for the principal and the school's staff. Although the summer provides a vacation respite for all employees, the ever-haunting principal's to-do list is a constant reminder of tasks that are incomplete and others that need immediate attention. In July the principal has myriad job expectations directed toward the closing of one year and the opening of another. The efficient elementary administrator is probably attending to the many key tasks, such as

1. monitoring curriculum-writing projects
2. reviewing all staff evaluations
3. analyzing disciplinary trends
4. reviewing standardized test score results
5. constructing the school calendar
6. meeting with PTA leaders
7. writing letters of welcome to new students
8. writing letters to new staff members
9. writing thank-you notes to staff members for their previous year's efforts
10. finalizing the hiring of new staff members for the upcoming year

These job essentials usually do not include directing one's attention to the bilingual population's unique needs. To that end the principal should meet monthly with the district's community liaison. If no such

position exists, the school's leader should place the topic of the Hispanic community on the staff agenda. Some proactive plans should
emerge from the meeting.

In the following paragraphs, the ideas discussed came from conferences with principals who seem to have a sincere concern for their
immigrant population. They believe that their fervor, once recognized
by the faculty, will make the bilingual population's needs a schoolwide
priority.

MEETING WITH THE DISTRICT'S SCHOOL-COMMUNITY LIAISON

Many of the subsequent topics could be an outgrowth of a meeting with
the district's school-community liaison. The principal should explore
areas to involve the entire school in activities that lend support to the
mission of the community liaison. Some of these would include

- the names and addresses of new Spanish-speaking residents
- a report on the activities of local Hispanic clubs
- the minutes of the liaison's meeting with church officials
- the liaison's impression concerning the number of students participating in summer programs
- programs and activities of the town's service clubs
- the number of Hispanic children who passed their subjects, who
  left school, or who received awards at graduation
- a discussion on what Hispanic children are doing if they are not in
  summer school
- feedback from the children about how they were affected by orientation programs, tutoring, and after-school activities
- the principal's invitation for the liaison to attend the PTA organizational meeting
- the sharing of ideas to enhance the involvement of parents in the
  school
- the liaison's report from visiting Little League officials and Scout
  leaders

These discussions were part of a California principal's meeting with
a Spanish-speaking community member who serves as a school-family

liaison. Both of the people said they meet monthly and their conversations were related to the service organizations in town, to the Catholic Church officials, and to other key community members. In the event of a serious incident within the Hispanic community, the two immediately formed a crisis committee to ensure that all residents would be apprised of the facts. The key citizens on the committee were all volunteers, and they met as needed and not necessarily on a regular schedule.

SUMMER SCHOOL

A number of strategies assist limited-English-speaking children in summer school. We recommend that a committee of teachers be formed to annually review and further develop a summer school program. The committee should consist of the school principal, the bilingual staff, the district's community liaison, and one or more members of the Hispanic community. It is simply applying the same techniques we use to improve the curriculum for every other subject area.

Minimally, summer schools should offer courses that help these children to improve their language skills. This should go beyond verbal techniques by additionally including written assignments. This first element of instruction should support the academic school program. However, the summer offers a multitude of options to assist children who need higher-level language skills. In one California district the bilingual committee presented many exciting initiatives during summer school, such as

- Conducting classes in English, social studies, mathematics, science, physical education, and art. In a team-teaching arrangement in English and social studies, classroom instruction was given by a certified subject-area teacher and a bilingual staff member. Both teachers recommended a similar program to be offered during the regular school year.
- Offering a reading program that had flexible hours and consisted of trips to local and school libraries to select and discuss books. There was no grade given since the staff's primary goal was to get children to read the high-interest, low-vocabulary books of their choosing. As their skills improved, the reading levels of their

selections were elevated. Book talks were encouraged and children learned many new vocabulary words.

- Scheduling field trips in which the children visited places of interest in the community, in addition to museums and parks. Prior to going to the sites, the students wrote letters asking for permission to visit. They also listed items they would look for during the trips and wrote them in both Spanish and English.
- Providing a guidance workshop to review their schedules for the new school year, answer any personal questions, and offer advice about homework, studying, and interaction with other children.
- Hosting a session at the end of summer school for the limited-English-speaking students to meet with the entire bilingual committee. This enabled the students to share their thoughts concerning the courses and programs the district offered in summer school.
- Holding a culminating luncheon with bilingual students and senior citizens in the high school. At this session, these senior role models discussed their experiences and reinforced the value of a solid education.

MEETING WITH PARENT-TEACHER ASSOCIATION LEADERS

It is not our purpose to review all of the items the principal and parent leaders would probably discuss at this initial planning session. One of the principal's priorities should be to institutionalize programs for the school's limited-English-speaking children and the involvement of their parents. Many PTA programs are quite adaptable for this purpose. International night, parent-child sports night, and an annual book fair are examples of activities that could involve all segments of the school and community.

PTAs rarely send invitations to their events in both English and Spanish. This could easily be accomplished by using Spanish-speaking parents or members of the teaching staff to translate these letters. This inclusion tactic could encourage foreign-born parents to attend more meetings.

If the PTA is involved in planning the first open-school night, its duties and functions could benefit from the involvement of the Hispanic parents. If Spanish-speaking parents are members of the PTA, they can serve as translators. Their involvement and assistance will be appreciated by those members of the community who speak little English. It is another attempt of outreach that should increase the attendance at this conference and at others held throughout the year. This thoughtful gesture will be a strong indication that they are an accepted part of the school's community and that their participation is valued.

In this regard, the principal should make certain that there are one or more community events that celebrate the diversity of the school's student population. We often use the term *inclusion* in contemporary education when speaking of integrating special education students into regular classrooms. The term should be applicable to the Hispanic population as well. Our Spanish-speaking students and their families will benefit greatly from being involved in PTA events and all aspects of school activities.

REVIEW THE SCHOOL'S DISCIPLINARY CODE

Two topics that are often overlooked in the writing of a school's disciplinary code are defamation and discrimination. In New York, one principal has included these terms under the heading of a disciplinary offense. He defines *defamation* as the "making of false or unsubstantiated statements about an individual or group that harms the reputation of that person or group by demeaning them." *Discrimination* is defined as "the use of race, color, creed, national origin, religion, gender, sexual orientation, physical appearance, academic ability, or disability as a basis of treating another person in a negative manner." In the disciplinary progression, infractions involving these areas are described as major offenses and incur appropriate punishments.

Much has been written recently about bullying. Through the ages, pupils have been teased by classmates. Adults rarely have viewed these mean-spirited acts as a serious problem. Since teasing, which often goes unchallenged, tends to escalate, administrators have finally recognized the damage it can inflict on innocent young people. Verbal abuse toward any student because of ethnic background inflicts pain and

should not be tolerated. These offenses should be spelled out in the
school's disciplinary code.

VISIT THE SUMMER SCHOOL BILINGUAL PROGRAM

All summer programs should be visited by the principal. In the context
of this book, our emphasis is on classes designed to assist children with
limited English-language skills. It is advisable for the principal to
invite the community representative and parent members of the bilingual committee to observe the program in action. The visit should
enable them to evaluate the initiative and make suggestions to improve
the program's offerings.

Unlike kindergarten show-and-tell presentations, these summer programs should be academically more challenging. The school's academic leader should observe the books and materials being used and
the quality of instruction the children receive. We are not recommending the elimination of field trips but would hope they are directed
toward instructional goals. If children are visiting places in the community, teacher-made worksheets should be developed to enhance the students' English vocabulary.

CHECK ON CURRICULUM-WRITING PROJECTS

Principals should familiarize themselves with the position statement of
the National Council for the Social Studies titled "Curriculum Guidelines for Multicultural Education." These 23 statements should be
included in the teachers' handbook to make certain that all staff members are exposed to the suggestions no matter what their subject area.
Just reading them provides a mini in-service course in bilingual education.

1. Ethnic and cultural diversity should permeate the total school
   environment.
2. School policies and procedures should foster positive multicultural interactions and understandings among students, teachers,
   and the support staff.

3. A school's staff should reflect the ethnic and cultural diversity within the United States.

4. Schools should have systematic, comprehensive, mandatory, and continuing staff-development programs.

5. The curriculum should reflect the cultural learning styles and characteristics of the students within the school community.

6. The multicultural curriculum should provide students with continuous opportunities to develop a better sense of self.

7. The curriculum should help students understand the totality of the experience of ethnic and cultural groups in the United States.

8. The multicultural curriculum should help students understand that a conflict between ideals and realities always exists in human societies.

9. The multicultural curriculum should explore and clarify ethnic and cultural alternatives and options in the United States.

10. The multicultural curriculum should promote values, attitudes, and behaviors that support ethnic pluralism and cultural diversity. *E Pluribus Unum* should be the goal of the schools and nation.

11. The multicultural curriculum should help students develop the skills necessary for effective interpersonal, interethnic, and intercultural group understanding.

12. The multicultural curriculum should help students develop their decision-making abilities, social participation, and sense of political efficacy as necessary bases for effective citizenship in a pluralistic democratic society.

13. The curriculum should be comprehensive in scope and sequence, should present holistic views of ethnic and cultural groups, and should be an integral part of the total school curriculum.

14. The multicultural curriculum should include the continuous study of cultures, historical experiences, social realities, and existential conditions of ethnic and cultural groups.

15. Interdisciplinary and multidisciplinary approaches should be used in designing and implementing the curriculum.

16. The multicultural curriculum should use comparative approaches in the study of ethnic and cultural groups.

17. The curriculum should help students to view and interpret

events, situations, and conflict from diverse ethnic and cultural perspectives.

18. The multicultural curriculum should conceptualize and describe the development of the United States as a multidirectional society.
19. Schools should provide opportunities for students to participate in the aesthetic experiences of various ethnic and cultural groups.
20. The multicultural curriculum should provide opportunities for students to study ethnic-group languages as legitimate communication systems and help them develop full literacy in at least two languages.
21. The multicultural curriculum should make maximum use of experiential learning, especially local community resources.
22. The assessment procedures used with students should reflect their ethnic and cultural experiences.
23. Schools should conduct ongoing, systematic evaluations of the goals, methods, and instructional materials used in teaching about ethnic and cultural diversity. (Banks, Cortés, Gay, Garcia, & Ochoa, 1991)

These guidelines are the most comprehensive list of multicultural program goals that we've found in examining numerous research studies. They serve as a model for every subject area's curriculum development. Achieving all these objectives is virtually impossible, but they are the ultimate target for caring staff and administrators. If these guidelines are not part of the teacher handbook, they would be a valuable attachment to any one of the principal's weekly memorandums to staff. They serve as a virtual in-service course.

Understanding the summer school teachers' objectives in teaching limited-English-speaking children will also allow the principal to focus the direction of the staff working on summer writing projects. Specific materials should be developed to enhance the summer school and regular school program. If field trips are to be taken to local business establishments, worksheets should be created to enhance the experience. These can be as simple as vocabulary words written in English and Spanish or as sophisticated as open-ended essay assignments.

A literature search that will help the academic needs of the course offerings and provide stories that increase cultural pride should be collated and added to the teachers' resource files. The development of a list of Hispanic heroes and current political leaders and their intellectual achievements will add to the staff's base of knowledge. The curriculum must not be left to the whim of each teacher. Just as the other subjects have extensive academic requirements, so too should our bilingual courses.

COMPOSE LETTER TO NEW FOREIGN-BORN RESIDENTS

A letter to foreign-born residents, of which an example appears at the end of this chapter, should be an annual greeting to newly arrived Hispanic parents. Given their hesitancy to become actively involved with the school administration and authority figures, the letter will begin the school's outreach to this segment of the population. The goal is clear. We want the parents of all our students involved in the school, its programs, and our community.

The school-community representative should have canvassed residents and real estate agents to develop a list of new families who might need assistance. In a small district in Florida, these letters are delivered personally by the school's representative to start a dialogue with new residents. Once a meaningful letter is generated, it can be reused and this annual task performed in minutes.

DEVELOP A COMMITTEE FOR AN ADULT-EDUCATION PROGRAM FOR BILINGUAL PARENTS

A committee for an adult-education program for bilingual parents is a relatively new part of the district's continuing-education program. Create the committee in July since its members should be informed of their mission. People who serve should receive an assignment to develop a list of suggestions to be included in this adult-education program. The specifics, which include meeting dates and topics, should be organized and advertised in August.

Committee membership should include the principal, community liaison, teachers, a PTA representative, and bilingual parents. The course content that will be developed does not obviate the regular adult-education program.

A pre-K program adapted from the Freeport, New York, school district will be discussed in chapter 15. It was developed with the assistance of a bilingual school social worker who was intimately involved with the parents of the community and the service agencies that are available to these community members.

OFFER A SUMMER SPANISH-CONVERSATION COURSE FOR ALL STAFF MEMBERS

In well-funded districts, a summer Spanish-conversation course should be part of the staff's in-service program. Teachers receive course credit that may be applied to salary adjustments. If this is not financially feasible, the course should be given gratis and be a requirement for all staff members. Let's pause for a moment and define *staff* and *faculty*. Faculty comprises teachers in the building, whereas staff designates everyone who works in the school. We are recommending that secretaries, hall monitors, custodians, cafeteria employees, and volunteers be offered the opportunity to take a conversational Spanish course when employed in the elementary school.

In this era of school security concerns, it makes sense to have all personnel who greet visitors to the school be able to speak a little Spanish. This makes the building user friendly, and parents who cannot speak English can receive simple directions to the main office and assistance in signing the school's visitor registration book. The procedure may not be part of the school's public relations program, but it certainly leaves a favorable impression on residents entering the building.

In the one school district on Long Island, we observed an in-service course being taught by an English-as-a-second-language (ESL) staff member who submitted the following 10 salient suggestions:

1. Pair students with a buddy, preferably one who is kind and sensitive to their needs or speaks the same language.
2. Have students sit where most of the teaching is going on.

3. Learn something about the student's background and share it with the rest of the class. Be careful not to foster stereotypes.
4. Make sure students feel like they belong by including them in all activities and lessons. Allow students to participate in class by giving them tasks to do, not necessarily requiring speaking.
5. Use as many visuals as possible. Pictures, posters, graphs, charts, maps, and diagrams help them to learn.
6. Speak at a normal loudness, but slow down and keep vocabulary and syntax simple. Require students to use a bilingual dictionary or thesaurus as a guide.
7. Emphasize and repeat main ideas. Use synonyms whenever possible.
8. Do not hesitate to reach out to parents, and remember that translators are available.
9. Maintain realistic expectations. Use alternative grading systems when appropriate.
10. Remember that ESL teachers are always available as resource personnel.

HIRING NEW STAFF MEMBERS

Schools in middle- and upper-middle-class communities have often failed to hire a large number of minority teachers. It is rare for their faculty members to reflect the religious, racial, and ethnic background of the United States today. We are not recommending that race or religious preference be involved in the hiring of staff. We do recommend giving additional consideration to a teacher who speaks Spanish or is a member of the community.

We open this area of consideration since more minority teachers are in communities with a large minority presence. It's easy to say that people prefer to teach in areas that reflect their race, religion, or heritage. However, it is clear that in hiring minority teachers we provide additional role models for both our Spanish-speaking students and their classmates. Many children have never had a Black or Hispanic instructor. This recommendation is another technique to eliminate stereotypes, since children often parrot biased statements they've heard on the street or at home. One principal with an integrated faculty told us that after an open-school-night program a parent said, "My son never told me that Mrs. Taylor was Black." That observation was priceless and said a great deal about the parent and the child!

If school principals truly believe in shared decision making, staff members will be a part of the interviewing committees. School administrators are aware of which faculty members possess the values we've been discussing, and they should be afforded the opportunity to be a part of the selection process. The principal whose vision of shared decision making is "I'll make the decision and then share it with my faculty" will never be truly effective in contemporary U.S. education.

The following chapters headed by the months of the school year end with letters to parents, written in English, which we recommend be translated into Spanish where appropriate. This form of correspondence is the principal's attempt to make the philosophical objectives of bilingual education practical and meaningful. Each piece of correspondence was culled from letters shared with us from principals across the country.

North Gables Elementary School
555 Main Street
Gables, Texas 12345
Jane Carter
Principal
Re Parent Orientation Night and Welcome to New Residents Letter

Dear Mr. and Mrs. Sanchez,

The entire staff of the North Gables Elementary School would like to welcome you to our school. We look forward to meeting you next month, when we will invite all new residents to visit our school for a tour of the building. I plan to be present and answer any questions you may have about your child's education. We will have several parents and teachers who speak Spanish available in case that assistance is needed.

We also will take the opportunity to introduce Ms. Carmen Garcia, who is our school-community representative. Ms. Garcia will be visiting your home to answer any of your questions and to inform you about the services she provides. Ms. Garcia is a resident of our town, and the members of the Spanish-speaking community often call upon her when they have any concern about their children. Her job was created by our board of education to help new residents to adjust to our school and the community.

The meeting will be held on Wednesday evening, August 27 at 8 p.m. We are holding the meeting in the evening to make it possible for our working parents to attend. We hope you will join us and become a partner in your child's education. We will serve coffee and cake after the meeting so that you can get to know your neighbors and school principal. Ms. Garcia will be available to help us all communicate more efficiently. The meeting will formally end at 10 p.m.

Children do better in school when their parents are involved in their education. We hope you will come to the meeting and also join our parent-teacher association (PTA). Members of the PTA will be present since they too want to meet you and invite you to their meetings.

Once again, it is a pleasure to welcome you to our school. I look forward to meeting you at our parent orientation night. In September we will host another event so that you will be able to meet your child's teacher.

Sincerely,
Ms. Jane Carter, Principal

Here is the same letter in Spanish.

North Gables Elementary School
555 Main Street
Gables, Texas 12345
Jane Carter
Directora

Estimados Sres. Sanchez:

El personal de North Gables Elementary School quisiera darles la bienvenida a nuestra escuela. El mes entrante durante la invitacion que le estamos haciendo, asi como a todos los nuevos residentes, tendran la oportunidad de visitar la escuela y hacer un recorrido por los edificios. Yo planeo estar presente durante su visita para contestarles cualquier pregunta que puedan tener acerca de la educacion de su hijo(a). Para su conveniencia, estaran presentes varies padres y maestros que hablan Espanol.

Aprovecharemos de esa oportunidad para presentarles a la Sra. Carmen Garcia que es nuestra representante en la comunidad. La Sra. Garcia visitara en su casa para responder cualquier pregunta e informarle acerca de los servicios que ella les puede proveer. La Sra. Garcia es residente de Gables y es regularmente consultada por los vecinos de habia hispana acerca de cualquier inquietud que puedan tener con sus hijos.

La reunion tendra efecto el miercoles, 27 de Agosto a las 8:00 p.m. Estamos teniendo esta reunion en horas de la noche para facilitarle la asistencia a aquellos padres que trabajan. Esperamos que ustedes se unan a nosotros en esta importante reunion. Terminada la reunion, les invitamos a quedarse unos minutos con nosotros para que puedan conocer a sus vecinos mientras disfrutan de una taza de cafe y pasteles que seran servidos.

Sus hijos obtienen mejores resultados de sus esfuerzos en la escuela cuando los padres se involucran en su educacion. Esperamos que asistan a esta reunion y se unan a la Asociacion de Padres y Maestros (PTA). Algunos miembros del PTA estaran tambien presentes para conocerles e invitarles a sus reuniones.

Nuevamente, bienvenidos a nuestra escuela y esperamos verlos la noche del 27 de Agosto a las 8:00 p.m.

En el mes de Septiembre tendremos otra reunion para que conozcan los maestros de sus hijos.

Sinceramente,
Ms. Jane Carter, Directora

CHAPTER 4

August: Researching Demographics and Initiating Home Contacts

To fail to plan is to plan to fail

—Anonymous

The books are now closed on the previous year. Vacations for school administrators are probably over, and each principal is quickly returning to an action orientation. There are so many school-opening matters that all other issues are put on hold. The first concern is do everything possible to guarantee a smooth opening of school. Each task must be completed prior to the first day of classes. They are listed here in no particular order, since they are all priorities:

- Prepare school-opening remarks for staff.
- Meet with all supervisors and teachers in charge of grade levels.
- Finalize teacher handbook.
- Complete school-opening packet for staff.
- Check master schedule and all teacher assignments.
- Conduct final building inspection with head custodian.
- Meet with PTA leaders.
- Review instructional goals for each teacher.
- Compose welcome-back letter to staff.
- Compose letter to parents concerning the opening of school and include
  - room assignments
  - transportation schedules
  - school hours
  - information about school lunch
- Prepare first weekly memorandum to staff.

- Send out letters to aides and monitors.
- Review substitute-teacher list.
- Revise staff directory.
- Plan new-teacher orientation program.
- Fill remaining faculty positions.
- Establish fire drill schedules.
- Check bells and public address systems.
- Write special letter to kindergarten and pre-K parents.
- Determine principal's own goals for the year.

To this imposing list of duties we add the principal's responsibility to the bilingual community. As we will detail in the suggestions that follow, it is relatively easy to integrate the needs of our limited-English-speaking students into the principal's action agenda. Our purpose is to remind administrators of the incredible impact minorities and foreign-born students will have on the future of the United States. We have discussed demographic implications in a previous chapter, but a recent article more fully illustrates the point.

It appeared in *Newsday*, a New York City newspaper, and discussed a company that produced Swingline staples. Some years ago the original owners sold the company to a large corporation called American Brands. When the Teamsters Local 808 replaced the former bargaining unit, they negotiated a new contract for the employees. After the process was completed, the written contract was translated into 21 different languages! Administrators should keep this story in mind as they attempt to address students' needs and determine their own priorities.

If further data is necessary, we submit table 4.1. It shows data from an immigration study recently completed by American Community Service ranking, by percentage, the foreign-born population in counties in the United States. The information is quite revealing.

Perhaps the most startling fact is the rapidity of change. In a 10-year period, from 1990 to 2000, the Queens County foreign-born Hispanic population increased by 36%. It is further justification for the selection of the Hispanic community as our exemplar for this text.

We can suggest numerous strategies to integrate actions and programs to assist the children and parents of the Hispanic community as

Table 4.1   Foreign-Born Population in Some U.S. Counties

Rank	County	Percent
1	Miami-Dade County, Florida	52.7
2	Queens County, New York	45.1
3	Hudson County, New Jersey	39.1
4	San Francisco County, California	38.2
5	Kings County, New York	36.1
6	Los Angeles County, California	35.6
7	Santa Clara County, California	35.3
8	San Mateo County, California	31.0
9	Orange County, California	30.4
10	Bronx County, New York	29.6

Source: National Conference of States Legislatures, n.d.

the principal goes through the to-do list. Of the principal's 20 tasks at least half of them are worthy of these suggestions.

PLAN YOUR SCHOOL-OPENING REMARKS TO THE STAFF

After the necessary thank-you to the staff for their previous efforts, the principal usually sets the tone for the new school year. It is an opportunity to inspire the faculty to reach for the next higher level of professional practice. In addition to each staff member's personal goals, there should be some schoolwide objectives that are mentioned. This is an exceptional opportunity for the principal to discuss some of the ideas developed in August by the PTA and the bilingual committee. Some of these specific plans can be formulated in the meetings discussed below. They should be presented to the faculty at the school-opening meeting.

MEET WITH GRADE-LEVEL SUPERVISORS

A meeting with grade-level supervisors before school starts assists with planning schoolwide grade-level events. One principal in Santa Clara, California, says she always has two or three activities that help to bring people together. She mentioned the three initiatives her shared-decision-making team are focusing on this year.

The first project has each grade level develop a list of famous people of different ethnic, racial, and religious groups. Obviously, there will be an emphasis on the contributions of the Hispanic population, but by including every other culture, the children will also learn an appreciation for all people. The second project is an international dinner that will be the culminating activity for the school year. This involves the children's parents and the entire staff. The third project is a lead-up to the international dinner. Prior to the winter recess, the children and their parents write and publish an international cookbook that will be sold as a holiday present in December. The children vote upon which charity to send the proceeds to from the cookbook sales.

It is easy to tie each activity to the goals of elementary education. Children will involve their parents, write at their own ability level, and be able to take pride in their family's contributions to the activity. As we will document in the principal's other planning activities, there are many community-wide projects that will achieve this mission.

FINALIZE TEACHERS' HANDBOOK

Few principals include an in-service section in their staff handbook. They do an exemplary job of detailing all of the necessary school rules and procedures. Including information such as the data we presented on population demographics might prove enlightening and informative, especially to our older staff members who may not have taken a college or in-service course in quite some time.

Following up on the suggestion of the principal from Santa Clara, we would include a minilist of famous people from many cultural backgrounds, with the hope that each teacher and class would add to the list. Examples include the following:

- Hispanic Americans
  - Franklin Chang-Diaz—astronaut, first Hispanic American in U.S. space program
  - Cesar Chavez—founder of United Farm Workers
  - Henry Cisneros—former secretary of Housing and Urban Development
  - Antonia Novello—former U.S. surgeon general
  - Katherine Ortega—former U.S. treasurer

- You may also use popular stars such as Roberto Clemente, Joan Baez, and Jose Feliciano
- Asian Americans
  - I. M. Pei—architect
  - Amy Tan—author
  - Daniel Inouye—U.S. senator
  - Maya Lin—designer of Vietnam Veterans Memorial
  - Ellison Onizuka—*Challenger* astronaut
  - You may also use Connie Chung, Kristy Yamaguchi, Pat Morita, and Michael Chang
- African Americans
  - Colin Powell—former general and secretary of state
  - Maya Angelou—poet
  - Carol Moseley Braun—former U.S. senator
  - Dr. Mae Jemison—first female African American astronaut
  - Douglas Wilder—former governor of Virginia
  - You may also use Jackie Robinson, Sammy Davis Jr., and Ossie Davis

These are clearly not exhaustive lists, but they should contribute to a positive mind-set for children and staff alike. We would expect the lists to grow and include other cultural groups and hope to see pictures of these citizens throughout the school and classrooms. Research reports outlining their lives are logical assignments for the upper grades.

We will make no attempt to list the other items in the handbook. When a principal includes these expectations and data, the handbook becomes a living document. Its distribution adds to the quality of education in the building and to the esteem the faculty feels for its leader.

MEET WITH PARENT-TEACHER ASSOCIATION LEADERS

This month is an excellent time to meet with the officers of the PTA. Among the agenda items should be the PTA's programs for the school year. We'll address only one activity, a community-wide event to celebrate the diversity of the student body. The event is also a means by which the principal educates the indigenous community members about the school and society's changing demographics.

One program, developed in a Suffolk County school district on Long Island, was Unity Day. The event took place toward the end of the school year, but every class was involved in a related activity. Ultimately, there was a series of events that included a fashion show of attire from parents' homelands, a student-written and -enacted play, an art poster contest, and a written pledge signed by every student and faculty member in the building. The pledge stated each person's commitment to preventing prejudice in any form.

We'd also recommend that the PTA invite Spanish-speaking translators to all of its events and adopt plans to reach out to members of the community for whom English is a second language. One district in New York City has an annual Foods of All Nations Luncheon to kick off their PTA membership drive.

REVIEW INSTRUCTIONAL GOALS FOR EACH TEACHER

Informing teachers about the major intercultural events being planned for the year affords them the opportunity to do some planning during the closing days of their summer vacation with respect to these activities. This might be done through the grade-level leaders, individual conferences, or the school-opening letter to the faculty. This tactic is recommended since it is the elementary school principal's expectation that the staff will go beyond the teaching of the three Rs.

To further pique their interest, the principal should inform them of the additions to the teachers' handbook that include statistics about the changing demographics of the U.S. school population and examples of famous people of different ethnic backgrounds.

PLAN NEW-TEACHER ORIENTATION PROGRAM

We will not attempt to enumerate the multitude of rules and requirements about which new teachers should be informed. These must be the principal's immediate priorities. As part of the orientation program, the building's leader should find the time to offer some in-service instruction about the school's changing population and the expectations the principal has for meeting the needs of the bilingual student body. Descriptions of their culture and parental attitudes should be part of the preparation of new staff members. This need is most urgent when new teachers come from a more affluent and stable community.

WRITE REGISTRATION ANNOUNCEMENT FOR NEW STUDENTS

Although the district usually includes new-student registration information in its newsletter, the school principal might want to place a similar notification in the local press or display posters in neighborhood business establishments. Here too, the message can be written in both languages.

MEET WITH THE BILINGUAL COMMITTEE TO PLAN PARENTING WORKSHOPS

The parenting workshop, which will be described in detail in our chapter on a model school district program, should do the following:

1. Provide parents with the skills needed to help their children succeed in school.
2. Share information about curriculum and school academic requirements.
3. Inform parents about extracurricular activities.
4. Help parents to read and interpret school reports and other correspondence.
5. Assist parents with their personal problems and social needs.
6. Exhort parents to get involved in school organizations such as the PTA.
7. Invite speakers of status in the community to participate in discussions.
8. Develop materials for parents to take home and use with their children.

PLAN A PROGRAM FOR PARENTS OF
KINDERGARTEN OR PRE-K CHILDREN

A program for parents of kindergarten or pre-K children is a type of community outreach intended to assist parents whose children are attending school for the first time. The description of the content of the sessions will also be discussed in our chapter on a model school district program. This effort would be educationally sound for any school, no matter what the makeup of their student population.

EVALUATE THE SUMMER SCHOOL'S BILINGUAL
PROGRAM

Meeting with the staff to determine the strengths and weaknesses of the annual summer school program should enable the principal to begin the improvement process. One procedure a Dade County school district uses is to have the staff members who will teach the courses the following summer meet and revise the curriculum in the spring of the school year. This is the one curriculum-writing team that is not employed in the summer since their revisions are needed for the summer. If an excellent rapport exists between the committee and the community's liaison, it's a good idea for the representative to share the children's reactions to the summer experience.

WRITE A SPECIAL LETTER TO PRE-K PARENTS

A letter to parents of pre-K children inviting them to a kindergarten orientation meeting is another letter that can be written in both English and Spanish. If we truly believe in reaching out to the more reticent foreign-language-speaking parent, this is a special opportunity to do so. It is another way that principals can convince new residents that they are welcome to the school and that there is a sincere desire for them to become involved in their child's education. The letter concerning the orientation meeting might look like the following:

North Gables Elementary School
555 Main Street
Gables, Texas 12345
Jane Carter
Principal
Re Special Orientation Meeting

Dear Parents,

Our school year is beginning on Monday, August 15, at 8:45 a.m. All of our staff members want your child to have a good learning experience at North Gables Elementary School. We want every student to learn and be happy to attend school. We also ask for the help of our parents since we believe there should be a school-home partnership in educating our children.

To assist our students who do not speak English fluently, we are going to invite them to visit the school the week before school opens. Ms. Garcia (our community liaison) and several parents who speak Spanish will assist me in helping your children find their classrooms and learn what they should bring to school every day.

Parents are welcome to attend the meeting. If the children are with babysitters that day, we would be pleased to invite them to attend. By giving the children the opportunity to visit before the start of school, we believe they will learn a little about our building and be more comfortable during the first day of regular classes.

Please remember the following:

- Welcome Day is Thursday, August 11, at 10 a.m.
- Children will be dismissed at noon.
- We will serve them milk and cookies when they arrive.
- Parents may stay and meet with Ms. Garcia from 10 a.m. to noon.
- The children will come home with a list of items they will need for the start of school.

We hope you will be able to attend the meeting. All of the members of the school-community committee will also be present to answer any questions you may have.

Sincerely,
Ms. Jane Carter, Principal

North Gables Elementary School
555 Main Street
Gables, Texas 12345
Jane Carter
Principal
Re Kindergarten Newsletter

Dear Parents,

All of the members of the North Gables Elementary School family are looking forward to meeting your children at the start of our new school year. We hope you had a wonderful summer and enjoyed a healthy and restful vacation. I'd like to share some important information with you in order for us to have an orderly start for our school year.

School will officially open on August 15, at 8:45 a.m. Attached to this letter is your child's bus pass. Written on the pass is the exact location and time for your child to meet the bus. On the first day the bus may be a little late, so please be patient.

Since our school lunchroom will not be fully operating, please send a lunch with your child. We will provide milk and cookies for the first day of school.

Kindergarten parents may want to attach their children's names to their clothing so that we can greet them and tell them where their classroom is located. We will have people available who speak Spanish to make sure we can assist the children who speak little English. We will do everything to help the children have a wonderful first day of school.

We also want parents to help with their children's education. Please do the following:

- Check their homework every night.
- Read with them daily and limit their TV time.
- Go to the library with them for books and attend the story hour.
- Come to school meetings with your child's teacher.
- Join the parent-teacher association and attend the meetings.

We are going to have some exciting programs during the school year. We hope you will join us for open-school night. We will send invitations to both events to you and your family. Call me if you have any concerns.

Sincerely,
Ms. Jane Carter, Principal

CHAPTER 5

September: Motivating Staff and Involving School-Community Committees

The great leader is he who the people say, we did it ourselves.

—Lao-Tsu

If the school opening is orderly and a calm educational tone is established, the principal's summer work schedule proved effective. As with Lao-Tsu's observation, everything worked so well, the principal's role went unnoticed. The mature leader views this as the ultimate compliment and does not feel slighted that his or her efforts went unnoticed.

The school-opening tasks are, at first glance, simply overwhelming. There are no unimportant duties. Every agenda item must be addressed to assure a school start that will instill pride in the staff and student body. The organized and caring principal will have completed the following major job expectations:

- planned and conducted the first faculty meeting
- held dry runs for the opening of school
- met with security staff, faculty, supervisors, and aides
- conducted the new-student and new-teacher orientations
- met with all cocurricular advisors and grade-level leaders
- reviewed expectations for custodial staff
- met with PTA leaders and planned the year's programs
- completed and distributed the teacher handbook
- double-checked the master schedule, teacher assignments, and room assignments

This does not include many of the more mundane required tasks that must be completed over the summer, such as checking if the public address system is operational, that safety signs are posted, that classrooms are properly equipped, and that all teacher duty rosters are completed.

This is a special month for our Hispanic community and the principal has an obligation that goes beyond the multitude of school-opening activities. Because it's so early in the academic calendar, many school districts simply overlook National Hispanic Heritage Month. The dates reserved for the celebration are from September 15 to October 15. With more than 37 million people in the United States of Hispanic origin, the celebration should be an opportunity, not a burden. With U.S. population reaching 300 million, it should be noted that citizens of Hispanic background will shortly account for 10% of our population.

Perhaps the immediate goals for the elementary school might best be presented in the principal's weekly memorandum. It should encapsulate the start-of-year expectations and the necessary planning for the first major school-community activity. It is the principal's attempt to focus the creative energy of the faculty and support its organizations for September and October.

Sample Weekly Memorandum
To: All Staff
From: Jane Carter
Date: September, Week 2

I want to thank the entire staff for the excellent manner in which each of you performed during our first week of school. Through your efforts our children were afforded a wonderful educational experience. The tone of the building was truly superior and our academic environment was a model of efficiency. You deserved the many accolades I received on your behalf from our parents. I'm proud of your professionalism and dedication.

The president of the United States recently announced the formation of a historic collaboration called Partners in Hispanic Education. The effort brought together the nation's leading Hispanic organizations, corporate leaders, and the members of the White House Initiative on Educational Excellence for Hispanic Americans. The goals of the organization are identical to our efforts to raise the expectation levels of our Hispanic students and parents.

Over the summer, I was able to meet with many of our school-related organizations to discuss a possible major activity that we could plan in order to take an active part in celebrating National Hispanic Heritage Month. I met with each of the following groups to gain their input:

- the parent-teacher association
- the school-community committee
- our building's shared-decision-making team
- the officers of the Hispanic American Club
- the service organizations consortium
- the adult-education committee

I was extremely pleased that, although I received their recommendations, every group felt that the professional faculty should decide the specific activity. This demonstrated their obvious respect for the staff and the belief that only the teachers could develop activities that would be appropriate for each grade level. The parents also mentioned that our classroom teachers would make sure that the projects were consistent with the district's curriculum goals.

I would like to share the input of each organization with you in the form of the brief minutes I took at their session so that a decision can be made about which activity we should pursue. Each grade-level leader will get the recommendations of their teachers, and at this Thursday's faculty meeting we will determine our project.

THE PARENT-TEACHER ASSOCIATION

It is a good idea to begin the school year with a major activity that would involve the entire school and community. The following possibilities might be considered:

- foods-of-all-nations day
- international olympics (athletic contests and songs)
- career day (to get children's parents involved as presenters)
- art and music of all nations (class and individual projects)
- songs and class skits (brotherhood theme)

Parents can volunteer to help with advertising the event and by raising money to help pay for materials and supplies. They may also indicate their willingness to assist the staff with decorations and refreshments for the event.

THE SCHOOL-COMMUNITY COMMITTEE

We've already discussed several activities that the school can consider celebrating, related to not only the Hispanic population but also the wealth of traditions brought to America by our multicultural citizens. If the PTA wanted to have an exciting program to kick off the school year, a schoolwide celebration of the Hispanic community's contribution to America might be educationally sound. Some suggestions are listed in the following.

- Display flags of all nations from which Hispanic Americans emigrated.
- Create list of basic vocabulary words studied by pre-K, kindergarten, and first graders in both Spanish and English. Examples include the numbers 1 to 10, colors, classroom items, and names of family relationships.
- Create lists of the Spanish names of American states and cities.
- Develop posters picturing famous people from the Hispanic community.
- Grade levels that study the age of exploration can prepare papers on famous Hispanic explorers such as Juan Ponce de Leon, Hernando DeSoto, Vasco Balboa, Juan Pizaro, and Hernando Cortez.
- The music department can honor Hispanic entertainers such as Tito Puente, Gloria Estefan, and Joan Baez.
- Physical education department members can create a display of major sports heroes, from Pele in soccer to Nancy Lopez in golf and literally hundreds of baseball players, including Hall of Fame members such as Roberto Clemente. The latter was also a great humanitarian who lost his life in a plane crash while taking food and clothing to quake victims in Ecuador.

The committee would recommend that the names and contributions of Hispanic Americans tentatively listed would be increased by staff members, students, and residents. The list could be continually enhanced and serve as an excellent database for everyone in the school and community.

SHARED-DECISION-MAKING COMMITTEE

The shared-decision-making committee would first approve kicking off the year with a major event. Consensus would be granted to honor our Spanish-speaking children since it was September and National Hispanic Heritage Month. Major concerns could be expressed about the timing of the event. Teachers might feel strongly that the staff should be given the opportunity to first establish class routines and get to know their children prior to planning for the schoolwide activity. The team might wish to establish classroom routines and suggest that the program be held in the latter part of October.

The team would also discuss several other items, listed here, that were not part of the upcoming celebration:

- open house—to inform parents that the evening is to discuss curriculum and not individual children
- new-teacher orientation—dates and topics to be determined
- major goal for the year—revision of report cards; this would probably be discussed in detail at the next faculty meeting

MEETING WITH HISPANIC AMERICAN CLUB

It would be valuable to get the Hispanic American club involved in the intended project as soon as possible. Members would probably endorse the activity since it is a vehicle to honor their heritage. The principal would ask for their support and involvement in the activity.

This type of meeting encourages mutual respect. The Hispanic and other immigrant community members would now realize that the school is attempting to assist their children. Often, teamwork replaces suspicion, and cooperation between the school and the community becomes the operational mode. The activity and the principal serve to convince the non-English-speaking families that their children are being educated by a caring school staff.

MEETING WITH THE COMMUNITY'S SERVICE CLUBS

Most likely the business community would be willing to support projects that would honor the Hispanic culture. They probably would not want to get involved in the selection of the program but would lend financial support, help advertise the event, and place posters in their stores. The principal's portion of the meeting would be highly anticipated. In a meeting with the community's service clubs an explanation should be given about the proposed activity and its academic significance. The principal might end the presentation with a word of appreciation for the service clubs' support and for all of their past efforts.

MEETING WITH THE ADULT-EDUCATION COMMITTEE

Members of the adult-education committee would be anxious to help in any way they could. They might involve several of the adult-education classes by developing material to include in some display. They might develop brochures and posters to help advertise the event. This committee's representatives ought to be sensitive enough to propose that the program include all segments of the community as well as the schoolchildren. The principal's participation should serve to motivate the members. The principal can thank them in advance for their input and support.

The principal's weekly memorandum should include the results of each committee's discussions. Extolling its support for the project and the school staff's ideas should be mentioned as well. Securing the community's approval would add to the enthusiasm for the project.

Principal's Weekly Memorandum and Upcoming Events

Thursday, September 12: faculty meeting in room 200 at 3:45 p.m. to determine our project and to discuss our first open-school night

Wednesday, September 18: open-school night

Thursday, September 19: meeting of shared-decision-making committee

Friday, September 27: submit lesson plans and dates for October field trips

Although it is merely a one liner in the weekly memo to staff, open-school night is a major event and must be planned in a meticulous manner. This is an opportunity for parents to meet their child's teacher. For many parents, it is their first visit to the school. Before discussing the unique methods used to approach the Hispanic community, the principal should complete the following tasks:

1. Prepare the PTA for the open house by sharing its purpose, date, and time.
2. Ask PTA volunteers to sell PTA memberships and serve refreshments.
3. Have class mothers call parents to remind them to attend.
4. Act as guides for new parents looking for rooms.
5. Offer to distribute first PTA newsletter to parents at the open house.
6. Prepare a PTA meeting-date schedule for distribution.
7. Write a letter of invitation to all parents.
8. Prepare welcoming speech for parents' meeting.
9. Meet with custodians to review cleaning plans.
10. Remind teachers to display student work and to enhance the appearance of bulletin boards.

For Hispanic parents, we would translate the letter of invitation to the open house into Spanish and provide Spanish-speaking guides to assist them during the evening's program.

North Gables Elementary School
555 Main Street
Gables, Texas 12345
Jane Carter
Principal
Re Open-School Night

Dear Parent,

We would like to invite you to the North Gables Elementary School to meet your child's teacher. The open house will be held Wednesday, September 18, at 7:30 p.m.

The purpose of the open house is twofold: first, to explain the curric-

ulum to parents and, second, to offer ideas and suggestions for helping students at home. When parents and teachers work together, children learn more!

We have invited our Hispanic liaison, Ms. Carmen Garcia, to attend
the meeting to help parents learn where their child's room is located.
Ms. Garcia will also be available to provide language assistance for
those who do not speak fluent English. Several other Spanish-speaking
community members will also be available to assist parents to make
the evening a success.

We encourage you to join our parent-teacher association (PTA). The
officers have planned many programs for you and have promised to
always have Spanish-speaking parents available to help you understand everything that is being discussed. PTA members will be sitting
at a desk in the front lobby to distribute the membership forms.

Our PTA will be serving refreshments in the school cafeteria. Please
join us at the end of the meeting, and I will introduce you to the officers
of the PTA. So put Wednesday the 18th on your calendar. We welcome
you to our school's family.

Sincerely,
Ms. Jane Carter, Principal

North Gables Elementary School
555 Main Street
Gables, Texas 12345
Jane Carter
Principal
Re Parenting-Workshop Invitation

Dear Parent,

We have a school-community committee to help our Spanish-
speaking parents and children become familiar with our teachers, curriculum, and community. Every year we ask our parents what we can
do to help them become more comfortable and more active in school
activities. This year we will offer a course for parents to give them ideas
about how to help their children with schoolwork.

Two of our bilingual teachers will teach the course. Mrs. Carol Rodriguez and Mr. John Russo will be joined by our community liaison, Ms. Carmen Garcia, to help parents with any problems.

The dates and topics are listed below:

- Wednesday, September 24, at 7:30 p.m.: information session
- Wednesday, October 1, at 7:30 p.m.: how children are taught English
- Wednesday, October 7, at 7:30 p.m.: how parents can help at home
- Wednesday, October 14, at 7:30 p.m.: where to find help with problems
- Wednesday, October 21, at 7:30 p.m.: homework and discipline

Please come and be a part of this wonderful program.

Sincerely,
Ms. Jane Carter, Principal

I will attend the Parenting Workshop set for Wednesday, September 24.

      Name of Parent _____

      Name of Child _____

Please have your child return this form to his or her classroom teacher, drop it off in the principal's office, or call the main office at 123–4567.

CHAPTER 6

October: Planning and Hosting the First Major School-Community Event

Great things are not done by impulse, but by a series of small things brought together.

—Vincent van Gogh

The principal is now focusing on activities that will sustain and enhance the collective energy of the faculty. Last month the staff selected a major school-community project, held its first open house, participated in a before-school faculty meeting, and formalized their routines for each class. The principal assisted the PTA in planning the year's program, began the new-teacher orientation program, met with all members of the nonprofessional staff, and evaluated the school-opening process.

In October there are a multitude of key tasks. The principal should be involved in the following activities:

- Host the site-based committee meeting.
- Meet with all grade-level leaders to affirm goals and priorities.
- Review instructional mandates for students in need of special services.
- Plan for the next faculty meeting.
- Observe all new teachers and nontenure staff members.
- Meet with school-community committee.
- Organize timelines and responsibilities for a Hispanic culture fair.
- Plan for first report cards and teacher-parent conferences.
- Plan Halloween alternative activities.
- Conduct fire and emergency drills.

For teachers, students, and parents, this is the second month of the school calendar. For the principal it is the fourth month, or one third of the way through the administrative work year. The plans carried out in July and August are essentially an administrator's academic-year requirements. For our purposes, energy must now be directed toward the integration of the needs of the Hispanic community into the October tasks of the elementary school principal.

SITE-BASED OR SHARED-DECISION-MAKING COMMITTEE

There are probably ongoing projects for the site-based or shared-decision-making committee to consider and possibly complete. These may have a priority since they are long-term ventures. The principal, as part of the team, must accept the committee-determined agenda. However, as a participating member of the site-based team, the school's representatives should be asked to demonstrate their support for the Hispanic culture fair. A simple request to include such a statement in the minutes of the meeting would serve to encourage the support of faculty and community members. As an example, an elementary school in Rhode Island sent a letter similar to the following to parents to garner support for a function to honor its Portuguese citizens.

North Gables Elementary School
555 Main Street
Gables, Texas 12345
Jane Carter
Principal
Re Minutes of the Shared-Decision-Making Council

Dear Parents,

Teachers, administrators, and parents will undertake several projects for the new school year. Our 2-year study of elementary school report cards has been presented to the faculty. After we receive your suggestions, we will finalize our recommendations and develop a prototype for a new report card. Our timeline will make it possible for us to have the new card ready for the next school year. Thank you for your participation in this important initiative, and we encourage you to return your suggestions promptly.

A second project is to upgrade the faculty room. This was undertaken not to merely address the staff's comfort level but to make it possible for teachers to call parents in private, to have a professional work area, and to house a library of up-to-date curriculum texts. The proposal has now been approved by the members of the district's central-office staff. A delay was caused by a concern that the phone would be used too often for personal calls. Approval was granted when it was agreed that all outside lines would be accessed through the principal's secretary. Teachers simply ask for an outside line, give their name, and say they are calling a parent. This will be made operational by February of this year.

Lastly, we would like to compliment the entire faculty on their selection of a community-wide program to honor our Portuguese residents. Every department and grade level has enthusiastically endorsed the project. We urge your complete cooperation with the coordinating committee and believe our efforts will do much to enhance our relationship with all members of our school and community.

Sincerely,
Ms. Jane Carter, Principal

Although Portuguese citizens are not considered Hispanic, the program coincides with the needs of the non-English-speaking community. Our principals have reported that in Mineola, New York, and Providence, Rhode Island, the Portuguese population has soared, as did the Hispanic population in Miami-Dade County, Florida; Queens County, New York; Hudson County, New Jersey; and San Francisco, Santa Clara, San Mateo, and Orange counties, California. This reinforces our thesis that all non-English-speaking new citizens need special assistance adjusting to speaking English and to U.S. culture.

MEET WITH GRADE-LEVEL LEADERS

Meeting with grade-level leaders affords the principal a unique opportunity to gain access to the entire staff through their team leaders. Putting all other issues aside, the manner in which each teacher and class will become involved in the Hispanic culture event should be a high priority, and its success will contribute to the spirit of the school and community.

Every team leader should be able to list possible projects for their grade. They should be not only age appropriate but also consistent with the mandated curriculum. Ideally, each team leader will return to the teachers of their grade and present a list of possible activities for their consideration. They should also allow the teachers to contribute their own ideas to gain a sense of personal involvement in the planning process.

We've detailed many of these possible activities in previous chapters. In response to a question we asked of principals at a major conference, we received reports of some unique activities concerning projects done throughout the nation.

- Each child wrote a biography about a famous Hispanic person.
- One class concentrated on the study of Hispanic women since their culture seems dominated by males.
- A class made a video of the historic contributions of Hispanic citizens that was then played at a local bank.
- Students made audio recordings of their grandparents describing life in the nation in which they were born. The children translated their stories into English.
- A class went to the library and the students found books about their native country. Their brief bibliographies were displayed by the local librarian in a decorated showcase with a map of the world.
- A primary-level class listed common words in English and Spanish that were distributed to parents and Spanish-speaking babysitters.
- One grade level held a luncheon in which parents of Spanish descent brought in samples of their favorite menus and recipes.
- A group of children edited an annual calendar to include multicultural holidays. These were placed on the district's calendar the following year.
- Several teachers wore Spanish shawls, hats, and other items of apparel to the school's international day.

- In one class, every student brought to a festival a person of Hispanic heritage in a different career field. There were doctors, lawyers, professors, teachers, nurses, laborers in the building trades, merchants, and fast-food restaurant employees. It was their hope that Hispanics would not be stereotyped.

The principal should now begin to work with the event committee to organize every facet of the day. For example, letters of invitation to parents and community members must be drafted and mailed promptly. It would be a sensitive touch to have these invitations signed by the PTA president and the faculty site-based team leader, as well as the principal. Additional invitations should be written to all local business owners, the local Hispanic organization, and city or village officials.

The principal should provide time for each class or grade level to set up their displays in a timely fashion. This necessitates a memo to the entire staff with the schedule and responsibilities detailed. Prior to this schedule being presented, the principal must meet with the custodial staff and present a physical plan outlining the need for tables, chairs, and public address systems and the location of waste receptacles. Custodians must be present to assist with emergency needs, to break down the displays, to take materials back to each classroom, and to do a complete cleaning of the area so that the school is ready for the following day of classes.

The principal's secretary might make personal calls to the leaders of all of the community service clubs to ask them to publicize the event and to have a delegation participate in the activities. This type of courtesy call should be extended to city officials and members of the school superintendent's central-office staff.

PLAN FOR THE NEXT FACULTY MEETING

Several principals employed unique strategies to enthuse their staff about the forthcoming Hispanic celebration. We were impressed by a principal from New York City. She invited her motivated teachers to address the faculty and explain what their classes would be doing at the event. She was convinced that staff members were more influenced by their colleagues than by her own exhortations. After the teachers enthusiastically discussed their class projects, many of the less involved staff members came to them to solicit ideas for their own classes.

The principal also has a rare opportunity to bring the purposes of the event to the staff. A motivational and educational presentation is recommended. Distributing the goals of the bilingual or ESL department would serve as a means to demonstrate to the faculty how the event will integrate the classroom objectives of the program. Another principal from a Long Island, New York, school district has several members of his staff tell stories of their parents' or grandparents' arrival in the United States. Many vignettes highlighted the trials and tribulations their ancestors experienced. The principal concludes the session by discussing the unique problems their own Hispanic population is confronting in contemporary America.

OBSERVATIONS OF NEW AND NONTENURE STAFF

The principal's highest priority is to assist new and nontenure teachers with their pedagogical skills. A postobservation evaluation conference of a live classroom performance led by the new staff member provides a format to discuss the lesson's strengths and weaknesses. After this is completed, the principal has an opportunity to discuss expectations for the teacher's involvement in the Hispanic celebration. The school leader may share ideas with the new staff member and emphasize why the program is essential for the members of our foreign-born community and their children.

Even when observing experienced teachers, the principal might discuss with them how they are planning to involve their classes in the October event. The principal's interest is a major motivational factor. If the building leader is thoroughly prepared, he or she may provide a list of possible classroom activities that are consistent with the goals of the event to each teacher evaluated.

MEET WITH SCHOOL-COMMUNITY COMMITTEE

The Hispanic celebration day should be a cooperative effort between the school and every organization represented by the members of the school-community committee. Each member is responsible to report on their organization's involvement. Each group must carry out the promises they made at the September meeting. For example, the Garden City, New York, Kiwanis International assisted a local district in the following ways:

- They made posters describing the event for every store owner to display.
- The local printer provided 1,000 copies of the program.
- They donated $500 toward the refreshments.
- Their officers and members attended the evening's festivities.
- As a special surprise, they established a $1,000 annual camp scholarship for a Hispanic child who was graduating from sixth grade.

The PTA will often contribute money, and its parents will volunteer to assist in setting up displays, preparing food, and cleaning up at the event's conclusion. They are an invaluable source of ideas since they network with other PTA organizations, have their own journal, and attend local, state, and national conferences.

We have major expectations for the school-community liaison. She will have the responsibility for visiting homes and local businesses to follow up on their commitments. She should report several times over the next 3 weeks to the principal to give a status report on her observations. The committee should also clarify her role during the evening program. The community liaison is the perfect emcee for the program since she is the most visible person in the community and knows most of the participants.

ORGANIZE TIMELINES FOR THE HISPANIC PROGRAM

The principal has had only a little more than a month to prepare for this major community-wide event. Meetings should be held with key communicators to review precise directions, times, and dates. The weekly memorandum to staff is the primary communication mode, but bulletin boards next to the morning sign-in sheet and notices in the teachers' room are also effective.

A principal in Connecticut displays a large countdown calendar above the teacher mailboxes and above the sign-in sheet. It simply says, for example, 14 school days until the big event. She started at 21 and went down to the last day, which she annotated "Planning completed— fun at last!"

HALLOWEEN

We have always organized an alternative activity to avoid trick-or-treating in the community. Often the PTA hosts a party with food, games, and prizes. The only admission fee is to sign a pledge that the student will not go out trick-or-treating after dark.

Since Halloween is celebrated on the last day of October, the school could plan the Hispanic international culture night on that date and thus eliminate many of the destructive incidents that often take place on the holiday. Children frequently attend school in costumes that day, and it would be more meaningful if they wore the dress of their ancestors. This would involve all ethnic, racial, and religious groups, as would the international feast that would end the evening's festivities. The entire community could advertise the event as an alternative to the destructive aspects of Halloween and a celebration of the district's diverse population.

North Gables Elementary School
555 Main Street
Gables, Texas 12345
Jane Carter
Principal
Re Invitation to the Hispanic-International Festival

Dear Parents and Community Residents,
   It has been said that the United States is "a nation of immigrants." With the exception of our Native American citizens, we have all come to these shores from another country. We are proud to be Americans, but we also have special feelings about our nation of origin. Where once the United States was called a melting pot, today's sociologists

liken our assimilation to a "mixed salad." This enables us all to be loyal Americans but recognizes that we continue to have pride in our past cultural traditions. The North Gables Elementary School is hosting our annual Hispanic-International Festival. We intend to honor our entire multicultural community.

The event has been planned with the help of our parent-teacher association (PTA), our community liaison, the chamber of commerce, our village officials, and the North Gables staff. We are inviting you to come to our school and help celebrate our diversity and to feel pride in your school and community.

The Event: Hispanic-International Festival
Place: North Gables Elementary School gymnasium
October 31
7:30 p.m.–10:00 p.m.

The North Gables High School Honor Society will provide babysitting services since we want parents with young children and preschool children to attend. Please feel free to bring older relatives and grand-parents since we want to include the entire family in our special program.

The PTA and several of our local business establishments are providing refreshments and many parents are bringing some of their home-cooked food specialties. It should be a family festival and feast of all nations featuring artifacts, videos, and food.

We want to thank all of the community groups who joined with our elementary school staff to help with the planning and advertisement for the festival. The evening will not be a success unless you and your family attend. Please come.

Sincerely,
Ms. Jane Carter, Principal

November: Using the Positive Tone From the First Activity to Reinvest in Future Efforts

I know I could never forgive myself if I elected to live without human purpose, without trying to help the poor and unfortunate, without recognizing that perhaps the purest joy in life comes from trying to help others.

—Arthur Ashe

If the principal's efforts to prepare for the first months of school were effective, a calm routine should now be the building's standard operating procedure. All staff members should be aware of their classroom duties and building assignments as they concentrate on instruction and the evaluation of each child's performance. This is the month for issuing the first report card, and all teachers should be prepared to grade students for course work and inform parents about their child's work habits and conduct.

Conducting kindergarten conferences, either with formal report cards or without, is extremely helpful for parents of the school's youngest children. A district in New Jersey has the pre-K and kindergarten teachers meet with parents and hand deliver the first report card. In this way they have an opportunity to discuss each child's progress and inform parents of how they can help at home. This is especially valuable for the limited-English-speaking families. Having the community liaison and Spanish-speaking PTA members available to assist during the conferences maximizes the effectiveness of two-way communication.

The principal's key tasks for the month include the following:

- disseminate of report cards
- devote more time to teacher evaluations
- review grades by teacher and grade level
- evaluate Hispanic-international day
- attend monthly PTA meeting
- organize school activities for Thanksgiving
- meet with student organization to encourage schoolwide service projects
- plan future activities with the school-community committee
- host shared-decision-making committee meeting
- start budget procedures for the following year

Prior to discussing the tasks that have particular impact for the Hispanic residents, the principal should explore ways to sustain the warm feelings engendered by the previous month's school-community event. With major holidays approaching in both November and December, a logical follow-up to the Hispanic-international day might be the publishing of an international cookbook. This project could involve the entire community and be used as a holiday gift. If the book is sold for a modest fee, the proceeds could be used to provide food baskets during Thanksgiving and gifts during the December holiday period to the community's needy families. We will discuss this project further when we demonstrate how many other school groups could be involved and how the principal could use the new initiative to continue the school's positive momentum.

REPORT CARDS

In elementary through high school, we strongly recommend a teacher-parent conference day to discuss the first report card and each student's progress. Up to now, the staff has met with parents only to describe the curriculum and to discuss classroom and homework procedures. Parents desperately want to learn how their child is adjusting to school and performing in his or her academic work.

Teachers recognize the importance of meeting with parents and are willing to offer suggestions to improve each child's performance. The staff recognizes that such conferences provide teachers with a valuable opportunity for them to learn from parents helpful things about each child, the family, and home conditions. We believe in the uniqueness of each individual and that one shoe does not fit all. Teachers must strive to design corrective strategies on an individual basis. Some parents may be given techniques to assist their child with basic skills, while another may learn that their child should be exploring the higher horizons of upper-grade-level material. This is clearly a limitation of report cards that can be overcome by scheduling the individual parent-teacher conferences. Wherever there is a foreign-language-speaking parent population in the community, eliciting the help of residents and staff members who speak the language is invaluable.

TEACHER EVALUATIONS

Part of the teacher-evaluation process includes a postobservation conference. At this time the teacher's performance is thoroughly discussed. Additionally, the principal can explore with the staff member several ongoing schoolwide projects. We'd suggest a request to have the teacher give a personal reaction to the Hispanic-day program and evaluate the quality of the contribution made by his or her class. It is a means to motivate the teacher about the opportunity for the class to participate in the cookbook publication and perhaps get it involved in another type of community service project. These seemingly minor conversations are effective ways to regenerate the interest of the faculty and to remind it of the principal's high expectations.

REVIEW GRADES BY TEACHERS

A principal in Massachusetts has her assistant principal develop a spreadsheet in which she lists the names and grades of every special education and foreign-language-speaking student. They then search for glaring inconsistencies or obvious grade discrimination in the student-evaluation process. Many times a simple conversation with a teacher will adequately answer any question that arises. However, there have been incidents when staff members maintained lower expectations for the foreign-born youngsters and never recognized this was a form of bias toward these children. The principal is not only the school's leader but the school's conscience!

ATTEND PTA MEETING

Attending a PTA meeting is a timely opportunity to get feedback from the active parents in the school. Evaluating the international day should be one of the principal's agenda priorities. Thanks should also be given to the members of the PTA for their participation and support of the project. The principal should mention accolades received from the community and the staff. It is another chance to compliment the faculty since staging the event early in the school year put additional stress on the classroom teachers.

Additionally, the principal should discuss the international cookbook that the staff was planning as a follow-up project to the Hispanic-international day. The objective is to get the PTA on board and to solicit its participation. Usually the PTA or the service clubs in the area will donate the funds to have the book published. Artistically talented parents might volunteer to illustrate the text. The principal is not only an organizer but also a coordinator.

EVALUATE THE HISPANIC-INTERNATIONAL DAY

We would recommend that the principal use both an anonymous form and a discussion method to evaluate the Hispanic-international day. Since staff are aware the principal was fully invested in the idea, they may be hesitant to criticize any aspect of the event. The weekly memorandum could start and end in the following manner.

Weekly Memorandum

I want to thank you for the high quality of your contributions to the success of our first annual Hispanic-international day. On your behalf, I have received many letters of appreciation, a plaque from the local Hispanic Club, and a huge number of complimentary phone calls. The involvement of your classes this early in our school year was a credit to your professionalism.

Please give your evaluative comments about the day's and evening's festivities. Since we've always sought to receive input that was credible and unbiased, the comments will be completely anonymous. We respect your daily time commitments and pressures, and we've designed a very simple evaluation form.

1. What was your overall impression about the activity?
2. Do you feel it is worthy of continuing in the future?
3. Was the timing too early in the year?
4. Do you feel it helped bring the community together?
5. Was it a positive experience for our students of limited English proficiency?

Please provide your responses on your own paper and submit it by next Friday. Thanks again for a job well done!

ORGANIZE THE SCHOOL FOR THE THANKSGIVING DAY HOLIDAY

The Thanksgiving holiday provides the school and students with many excellent community service projects. School clubs and organizations can sponsor food drives for needy families who reside in the school district. Usually principals maintain confidential lists of families who could benefit from food, store gift certificates, and donated turkeys. Deliveries are made when school is in session to avoid embarrassment to the children.

Upper-grade and secondary school classes often host in-school Thanksgiving Day meals for senior citizens. They may also invite the youngest children in the school and explain the history of the holiday. Elementary students dressing as Pilgrims and in the traditional garb of Native Americans can add a historical touch to the festivities.

Thanksgiving is a truly U.S. holiday and all children should benefit from its celebration and the unifying effect it has on the school and community. Foreign-born youngsters should learn its origins as part of the social studies curriculum. It is easy for the staff to assimilate the holiday into their instructional goals. Writing stories about early Americans and drawing pictures of the everyday life of the colonists makes learning fun and meaningful.

MEET WITH THE STUDENT ORGANIZATION

Children are eager to get involved in projects and activities. The principal will find them relatively easy to motivate. The following agenda for a student council meeting submitted by a principal from Minnesota speaks for itself:

- Get student reaction to our first major schoolwide project.
- Ask for volunteers for parent-teacher conference night.
- Discuss the logistics of the Thanksgiving food drive.
- Secure a list of students who speak Spanish to help new students, assist during the registration process, and guide parents to rooms during the conference night.
- Set up a separate community service committee to develop activities to help others throughout the school year.
- Seek volunteers to tutor non-English-speaking classmates.
- Determine the criteria for one or more community service awards to be given at graduation.

MEET THE SCHOOL-COMMUNITY COMMITTEE

The school-community committee should involve your shakers and movers. Most educators believe that if the school is coasting, it can only go downhill. The cookbook project is probably a good follow-up to the Hispanic-international day. Hopefully this momentum will carry the school through the end of December. The committee should explore proposals of other possible unifying activities to begin in January. These ideas will be discussed in the January chapter.

The principal should provide the committee with the list of 101 activities developed by the Anti-Defamation League with which we ended chapter 2. The suggestions should be made available to the school's shared-decision-making committee for consideration. A Massachusetts principal appended it to his weekly memorandum to motivate his staff to develop a major project for the second semester. One can readily see how the search for the new project can become a shared-decision-making activity for the entire faculty and all schoolwide departments, organizations, and committees.

The school-community committee should fully evaluate the Hispanic-international day activities. Its recommendations are important. The comments of the school's staff should be heeded since they can be insightful and are often the most educationally meaningful. They may feel that having both a day and evening celebration made teaching the regular curriculum difficult. Their classroom instruction may have been interrupted by noise in the halls, moving of furniture, or too many obtrusive parents and adult helpers in the building. Among the principal's highest priorities is the maintenance of a businesslike academic tone in the school. The enthusiasm for a project must never overshadow the school's primary responsibility, which is to educate all of the children by ensuring adequate time for grade-level curriculum instruction.

SHARED-DECISION-MAKING COMMITTEE

The members of the shared-decision-making committee will likely provide the most accurate evaluation of the Hispanic-international day program. If the committee members believe in their mission, they should discuss a detailed appraisal of the day and the preparation leading up to the event. The opinion of this committee should carry additional weight in determining whether the event should become annual and whether the school should develop follow-up activities to maximize the impact of the experience. Other selected agenda items would include all of the following:

- exploration of additional school-sponsored initiatives
- a vote to support the cookbook project
- evaluation of the teacher-parent conference night
- discussion of report card timelines and evaluation of departmental grades
- consideration of year-end faculty celebration for December
- general concerns of faculty members, parents, and aides

It is imperative to remind the entire staff about the importance of parental involvement in the school. It is a responsibility that should not be taken for granted. The following feelings are from a New York City principal's weekly memorandum to her staff.

She noted that New York City has a history of missed opportunity when it comes to engaging parents and residents in the efforts to turn troubled schools around. Suburban educators know by heart what appears to elude us: You can't run a successful school without community and parent participation.

If only all public schools could be fixed from City Hall, we'd be in good shape. But they can't. Strides in school improvement are more likely to be sustained when parents and communities are united with administrators. Governance reforms in the past changed structures, but seldom created the deep, sustained relationships between the schools and communities that actually improved public schools. We all know that students whose parents are involved in their education achieve higher levels than those whose parents are not. Schools with a strong parental and community group presence create a culture of success that attracts additional social investment.

The principal ended her memorandum by reminding her staff of the value of their partnership with the parent association, the school-community committee, and their own shared-decision-making committee. When talking about their school she mentioned that all descriptors begin with *we*, *our*, *ours*, *us*. The memorandum ended with the phrase, "Partners in Education is practiced here!"

North Gables Elementary School
555 Main Street
Gables, Texas 12345
Jane Carter
Principal
Re Request for Recipes for International Cookbook

Dear Parents,

Our recent Hispanic-international day celebration was a huge success. The event brought the entire community together, and it was wonderful to observe how much we were able to learn about the diverse cultures of the families who reside in our school district. The day's activities generated a warm feeling of community spirit.

In attempting to maintain that sense of togetherness, the parent-teacher association, our community-school committee, and the staff of North Gables are undertaking another project and want to encourage your participation. We are going to write an international cookbook and include the favorite recipes of our residents. We believe it is a way to preserve old family favorites and share them with the people of other ethnic cultures.

We have received generous donations from the Rotary Club and our own parent-teacher association to fund the publication of the book. We plan on selling them in the near future and will use the profits to assist our community's less fortunate members.

Kindly submit recipes with an accurate list of the ingredients and clearly written directions. Remember to include the country of origin and your name. Thank you in advance for your participation in this project.

Sincerely,
Ms. Jane Carter, Principal

Recipe Submission Form (Please Print)

Your Name: _____ Home Phone #: _____

Name of Recipe: _____

Ingredients:

_____

_____

_____

Food Preparation Instructions:

_____

_____

_____

_____

Please return to your child's teacher or to the school's main office.

North Gables Elementary School
555 Main Street
Gables, Texas 12345
Jane Carter
Principal
Re Report Card

Dear Parents and Guardians,

Attached to this letter you will find your child's first report card for the school year. It is an evaluation of your child's grades, effort, and conduct. Please read all three comments since your student's grades are often affected by the way he or she behaves in class and how he or she prepares for school.

We recommend that parents sit down and discuss every grade and comment with their child. This conversation demonstrates to your child that you value the importance of his or her work in school. We encourage parents to ask their children about what they did in school each day and to check their child's homework before it is submitted to the teacher. Parents are always their child's first teachers.

We have scheduled a parent-teacher conference night on Wednesday, November 17, to begin at 7 p.m. since we want to have an opportunity to discuss each child's progress with parents. If you have any questions, we hope to address them during the meeting. However, if you feel the content of the report card you are receiving today needs immediate attention, please call the principal's office. We will have the teacher call you.

Even if you are perfectly satisfied with the results of your child's report card, we encourage you to attend the parent-teacher conference evening. After the conferences you will have an opportunity to meet with our parent-teacher association members who will be serving refreshments. These parents schedule meetings throughout the year that we urge you to attend. It is another way for you to learn about our school and the district's programs. We hope you'll join us and be a partner in your child's education.

Sincerely,
Ms. Jane Carter, Principal

CHAPTER 8

December: Capturing the Holiday Spirit to Enhance Student Camaraderie

Tell me, I forget. Show me, I remember.
Involve me, I understand.

—Ancient Chinese proverb

Principals should attempt to keep the school's staff and student body focused on academics since the forthcoming holiday period can present distractions. The holiday concert must not be allowed to interrupt the building's academic tone. The principal's organizational activities, enumerated later, help to maintain instruction as a priority.

One of the school's major events is the holiday concert. With elementary school auditoriums generally being of limited seating capacity, principals have been forced to either have more than one performance for different grade levels or host the concert in the secondary school's auditorium. Precise planning must occur since the school's administration needs to consider the following:

1. Minimizing classroom interruptions and allowing for adequate rehearsal schedule.
2. Discussing the program's content.
3. Arranging for transportation to and from the secondary school for children, staff, and instruments.
4. Providing appropriate supervision for students not performing and those waiting to perform.
5. Adjusting class periods and the lunch schedule, if the program is held during the day.
6. Arranging supervision and ticket-taking assignments.
7. Writing letters of invitation to parents and community members.

8. Checking out the secondary school's auditorium, public address system, restroom locations, and stage settings.

In item 2, we mentioned that the principal should discuss the musical content of the concert with members of the department. Often the program's degree of religious content causes controversy rather than the solidarity that was intended. It's helpful to remember that we in the public schools should not favor one religion but teach a tolerance for all. Knowing residents' attitudes is helpful in making this decision. With the magnitude of program possibilities, we must strive not to offend any segment of our community and possibly cause hurt feelings instead of the togetherness we had intended.

This is also a high visibility month for the school since many parents will attend the concert. Add to this the holiday book fair and the volume of visitors will increase dramatically. Certainly a meeting with the custodial staff to address the appearance of the school's entrance, halls, and restrooms is recommended. Classroom teachers should be reminded to upgrade their bulletin boards and the overall appearance of their classrooms.

In several of the December responsibilities, we will note, the school's leader has an opportunity to motivate the staff and community organizations to develop a new project to sustain the seasonal feelings of goodwill and ensure that worthwhile curriculum objectives make it academically viable.

The key tasks for December include several responsibilities that are essential for the reopening of school in January following the holiday vacation. Perhaps the most important is to meet with the head custodian and develop work assignments to be accomplished over the winter recess. When students and staff return for the new calendar year, the building will be clean and several painting and construction projects will enhance the school's appearance. Other key tasks include the following:

- review budget proposals
- complete fire drills and send verification to the central office or the state
- schedule monthly faculty meeting

- assist sunshine committee with holiday party
- maximize number of classroom observations
- preview holiday concert selections
- host school-community committee
- meet with shared-decision-making committee
- attend holiday parties held by community's service clubs
- conduct locker and classroom cleanups
- meet with PTA leaders or attend their meeting
- design spring testing schedule

Sometimes it's more difficult to decide upon a logical follow-up event than it is to develop the original activity. The success of the Hispanic-international day warrants another major initiative that will build upon the school-community spirit it engendered. In discussions with the faculty, school-community committee, and PTA leaders, the principal should be prepared to place this item on each meeting's agenda.

Prior to participating in any of the December meetings, the principal must do some homework. Reviewing materials from some multicultural educators, historians, and organizations should help provide suggestions. Some of the following books should be part of the teachers' reference library since they can provide excellent insights and ideas:

Banks, J. A. (1997). *Teaching Strategies for Ethnic Studies.* Boston: Allyn & Bacon.

Banks, J. A., and C. A. M. Banks. (2001). *Multicultural Education.* New York: Wiley.

Booth, A., and J. Dunn. (1996). *Family-School Links: How They Affect Educational Outcomes.* Mahwah, NJ: Erlbaum.

Comer, J. (1995). *School Power: Implication of an Intervention Project.* New York: Free Press.

Goodlad, J. I. (1984). *A Place Called School: Prospects for the Future.* New York: McGraw-Hill.

Henderson, A. T., and N. Berla. (1994). *A New Generation of Evidence: The Family Is Critical to Student Achievement.* Washington, DC: National Committee for Citizenship Education.

Marshall, P. L. (2002). *Cultural Diversity in Our Schools.* Belmont, CA: Wadsworth/Thomson Learning.

Manning, M. L., and L. G. Baruth. (2004). *Multicultural Education of Children and Adolescents*. Boston: Allyn & Bacon.

Schneider, B., and J. S. Coleman. (1993). *Parents, Their Children, and Schools*. Boulder, CO: Westview.

In perusing some of this material, and prior to attending the December meetings, the principal should prepare a list of suggestions of possible schoolwide activities. It's the school leader's responsibility to promote events that are educationally sound and meaningful to the community. A principal from Providence, Rhode Island, shared her list of multicultural events that she keeps in her summer to-do folder:

1. Develop a list of all ethnic holidays and include them on the school district's calendar.
2. Establish a diversity or multicultural club to host monthly events.
3. Create an intergenerational club in which students videotape senior citizens' stories about why they came to America.
4. Hold a concert of songs of all nations.
5. Have each class adopt a foreign country and create a display about its customs.
6. Have an international olympics that includes dance, songs, and athletics.
7. Have teachers sponsor a poetry contest with a multicultural theme.
8. Develop a list of residents, teachers, and students who are willing and able to discuss their family's heritage.
9. Publish an international newspaper with articles about the many ethnic backgrounds of the students and residents.
10. Have each class write a skit about diversity to be performed at a grade-level assembly.
11. Develop a hall of fame depicting famous residents or historical figures who did something to benefit humankind.
12. Have each class write to pen pals in different communities and culminate the project with an interschool party.
13. Host an international film festival to be shown during lunchtime and to be discussed in class.

14. Design a multicultural quilt for permanent display in the school.
15. Develop a cookbook by getting recipes from the entire community.
16. Establish a human rights award for graduation and have the qualifications of all candidates read at an assembly program.
17. Have a walk- or run-against-hate event. Children should get sponsors and contribute money to a community cause or food kitchen.
18. Host a community-wide human rights day.
19. Build a float for the homecoming parade that celebrates the school population's diversity.
20. Have an international food festival with ethnic entertainment.

FACULTY MEETING

With approximately 15–17 school days in the month, the faculty may be feeling the loss of instructional time. The school concert and the necessary rehearsal schedule disrupt classroom instruction. If we add the holiday book fair and the hall traffic it generates, most of the staff will not be too receptive to discussing long-range suggestions. The principal would do well to provide each teacher with the list of 20 suggestions and inform them that the decision on future events would be made in January. As we have stressed, the academic tone of the building is the principal's highest priority.

Once the decision is put on hold, it's appropriate to discuss holiday classroom parties. All should be held after school hours to ensure they are consistent with our primary goal. Faculty celebrations may be considered and these activities should be held off school grounds at a restaurant or other facility. Finally, the principal should provide a message of appreciation for the staff's efforts during the first 4 months of the school year.

SCHOOL-COMMUNITY COMMITTEE

After reviewing the year's events, plans should be discussed for January through June. The principal should remind the school-community committee members about the winter concert and the book sale being sponsored by the PTA. A full discussion should be held on possible follow-up activities for the second semester. The principal could elicit ideas from committee members and provide a list as input to the discussion. We recommend that the principal set certain requirements during the selection process. The most important criteria is that the activity be able to include curriculum objectives for each grade level. In general, the faculty will support events that are consistent with the subject matter they are teaching in the classroom.

The principal should impart to the committee the desire of staff members to hold new events to a minimum so they have sufficient time to prepare their students for January examinations and state-mandated achievement tests. An event in March or April, followed by a culminating activity in June, might be their recommendation.

One example of an activity that would meet the criteria might be an international olympics. The first part would be a celebration of music and dance during the spring concert. Each grade level could take responsibility for some aspect of the event. There could also be an evening event for the residents of the community.

At an assembly in February, each class would select the country it would represent in both music and dance and later as an olympic team. The actual olympics would be held in June as the school's culminating activity. In this way, there would be an opportunity for individual and class participation in each event. This will enable students to begin their research concerning the country they will represent.

PTA BOARD MEETING

At the PTA board meeting the agenda would include the book sale, disbursement of cookbook sales revenue, and future school events. The principal would remind the PTA members about the winter concert and advise them about minimizing disruption of classes during the book-sale week.

The recommendations of the school-community committee would be shared with the PTA and, it is hoped, receive its endorsement. It is the principal's obligation to sell the program. Two strong reasons to support the events are that they will minimize any impact on the day-to-day instructional tone and that they will provide areas of curriculum for each grade-level class to use in its preparations for the olympics.

North Gables Elementary School
555 Main Street
Gables, Texas 12345
Jane Carter
Principal
Re Winter Recess

Dear Parents,

We have just completed 4 very rewarding months of our school year. The children were able to participate in many programs that brought our school and community together. Our Hispanic-international day was both joyful and meaningful to all of our residents. The winter concert gave us the opportunity to demonstrate the extraordinary talents of our students. The audience attested to the fact that it was a source of pride for our parents, children, and faculty.

All of us at North Gables Elementary School want to wish you a happy and healthy holiday and the best of luck in the new year. We are fortunate to work in such a caring community. When we encouraged your participation in school activities, you took every opportunity to become involved in your children's education. Our PTA has hosted programs that provided information and advice, and it was rewarded by a large attendance at every meeting. It was one of our parents who suggested we translate our letters home into Spanish, and this increased the participation of our Hispanic community in school activities. The feeling of teacher-parent cooperation has been a highlight of the first semester.

School will begin again on Monday, January 3. During the holiday period, we hope you will take advantage of the suggestions of our faculty and school-community committee and visit our local library. If you encourage your child to read, it will help him or her to improve in school. This is a chance for the family to become a true partner in your child's education.

We look forward to seeing your child on January 3. Again, we wish you the best of health and happiness for the new year. It is a joy to work with such a caring community.

Sincerely,
Ms. Jane Carter, Principal

CHAPTER 9

January: Involving Students and Staff in Planning Second-Semester Events

There are three kinds of administrators. One who makes things happen. One who lets things happen and a third who wonders what the heck happened.

—Robert Spillaine

The end of January concludes the first half of the academic year. With the vacation period concluded, the principal's first priority is to reestablish a businesslike tone for the school. There should be clear expectations for the staff and student body. Verbalizing second-semester goals via the public address system and frequent visits to classrooms are effective techniques to revitalize everyone in the school.

Some mention should be made about the life's work of Dr. Martin Luther King during the month. The national holiday celebrated in midmonth was established to honor his efforts to improve race relations in the United States. His work was akin to our attempt to reach out to the foreign-born parents of our community. A speech delivered on the public address system or a reminder to teachers to mention his contributions via the weekly memorandum would be a minimal expectation.

Each teacher is probably employing similar strategies with their own classes. In just a few weeks midyear testing will be scheduled and in many states achievement examinations are also mandated. Principals and teachers operate in the present while continuing to develop future long-range plans. With the pressure of preparing report cards and their timely distribution to parents, most faculties will appreciate putting major events on hold for a month.

In addition to the usual meetings of the PTA, shared-decision-making committee, school-community committee, and the monthly faculty meeting, the principal has several other major duties. All of the following responsibilities must be completed or remain works in progress:

- Continue to conduct staff observations.
- Plan for the distribution of report cards at the end of the month.
- Make preliminary decisions on whether to rehire nontenure staff members.
- Finalize budget requests and prepare for budget defense with central-office staff.
- Continue faculty in-service courses and new-teacher orientation program.
- Develop principal's presentation for the monthly PTA meeting.
- Complete midyear nonprofessional staff evaluations.

While addressing these major responsibilities, the building leader has to keep in mind that the school's momentum is usually fueled by the passion of its principal. While handling all of January's key tasks, the principal must develop a plan to motivate the kickoff for the second semester's major event. If the strategy is effective, the classroom teachers will follow the lead and infect their students with enthusiasm. The long-range plans of building-related committees should include a February selection of a country's name by each class, an April spring concert featuring songs and dances of the selected nation, and a June culminating olympic athletic event, entrance parade, and cheering contests.

As a possible means to stimulate discussion, one might send each class a list of all of the countries that are members of the United Nations. This was done in the Hampton Street School in Mineola, New York. The principal included the following message along with the names of the nations.

School Olympics News
To: All Teachers
From: Principal Carter

WHAT NATION WILL YOUR CLASS REPRESENT IN OUR SCHOOL'S OLYMPICS?

Next month every class will select a country in the world as part of our olympic celebration in June. The country will become your team name in a series of future events. Here is the tentative schedule.

1. Team names will be chosen next month (February).
2. During March all classes in each grade level will compete in a song or dance contest to decide which class will represent the grade at the school's spring concert. The songs and dances must be from the country your class represents.
3. In April's spring concert, the winning class on each grade level will perform for our parents, residents, and student body.
4. In June we will have an olympic event. This will be composed of a variety of athletic contests. We have added a cheering contest for each class to demonstrate the talent of your class and school spirit. In addition, each class will enter the athletic field in a parade of nations and will be judged on the costumes and uniforms your class creates.

The following countries are current members of the United Nations.

Afghanistan	Argentina	Bahrain
Albania	Armenia	Bangladesh
Algeria	Australia	Barbados
Andorra	Austria	Belarus
Angola	Azerbaijan	Belgium
Antigua/Barbuda	Bahamas	Belize

Benin

Bhutan

Bolivia

Bosnia/
   Herzegovina

Botswana

Brazil

Brunei

Bulgaria

Burkina Faso

Burundi

Cambodia

Cameroon

Canada

Cape Verde

Central African
   Republic

Chad

Chile

China

Colombia

Comoros

Congo

Costa Rica

Cote d'Ivoire

Croatia

Cuba

Cyprus

Czech Republic

Democratic
   Republic of the
   Congo

Denmark

Djibouti

Dominica

Dominican
   Republic

East Timor

Ecuador

Egypt

El Salvador

Equatorial Guinea

Eritrea

Estonia

Ethiopia

Fiji

Finland

France

Gabon

Gambia

Georgia

Germany

Ghana

Greece

Grenada

Guatemala

Guinea

Guinea Bissau

Guyana

Haiti

Honduras

Hungary

Iceland

India

Indonesia

Iran

Iraq

Ireland

Israel

Italy

Jamaica

Japan

Kazakhstan

Kenya

Kiribati

Korea, North

Korea, South

Kuwait

Kyrgyzstan

Laos

Lebanon

Lesotho

Liberia

Libya

Liechtenstein

Lithuania

Luxembourg

Macedonia

Madagascar

Malawi

Malaysia

Maldives

Mali

Malta

Marshall Islands

Mauritania

Mauritius

Mexico

Micronesia

Moldova

Monaco

Mongolia

Morocco

Mozambique

Myanmar (Burma)

Namibia

Nauru

Nepal

Netherlands

New Zealand

Nicaragua

Niger
Nigeria
Norway
Oman
Pakistan
Palau
Panama
Papua New Guinea
Paraguay
Peru
Philippines
Poland
Portugal
Qatar
Romania
Russia
Rwanda
Saint Kitts/Nevis
Saint Lucia
St. Vincent/
   Grenadines
Samoa
San Marino
Sao Tome and
   Principe

Saudi Arabia
Senegal
Serbia and
   Montenegro
Seychelles
Sierra Leone
Singapore
Slovakia
Slovenia
Solomon Islands
Somalia
South Africa
Spain
Sri Lanka
Sudan
Suriname
Swaziland
Sweden
Switzerland
Syria
Tajikistan
Tanzania
Thailand

Togo
Tonga
Trinidad and
   Tobago
Tunisia
Turkey
Turkmenistan
Tuvalu
Uganda
Ukraine
United Arab
   Emirates
United Kingdom
United States
Uruguay
Uzbekistan
Vanuatu
Venezuela
Vietnam
Yemen
Zambia
Zimbabwe

Teachers should begin a discussion with their classes to determine which countries they will choose to represent. To assist you during your deliberations, the school-community committee will share with us the results of a recent survey it completed. The purpose of the study was to discover how many foreign countries our parents and grandparents listed as their original homeland. The outcome was amazing: in a school of 570 students our parents came from 36 different countries. In the United States, we are all able to maintain pride in our family's heritage and also be considered loyal citizens of our country. We want to thank the committee for the information and offer it to all classes to consider as they go through their decision-making process.

If a class selects a country that was the homeland of a local resident, there is the potential for some interesting assistance. The parent could come to school and tell the class about why he or she immigrated to the United States and teach some songs or phrases in the country's language. He or she may even be helpful in demonstrating a dance indigenous to his or her original homeland. The resident could be a helpful educational resource.

RESULTS OF THE SCHOOL-COMMUNITY COMMITTEE'S SURVEY

Albania	Israel
Algeria	Italy
Austria	Japan
Bangladesh	Korea, South
China	Laos
Colombia	Mexico
Cuba	Pakistan
Czech Republic	Panama
Ecuador	Peru
United Kingdom	Poland
France	Portugal
Germany	Puerto Rico
Haiti	Russia
Honduras	Somalia
India	Spain
Indonesia	Ukraine
Iran	Vietnam
Ireland	West Africa

The committee made some observations that I'd like to share with the faculty and student body. The immigration from Europe, with the exception of recent arrivals from Russia, the Ukraine, and Albania, came mainly from second- and third-generation

Americans. The Hispanic and Asian population make up the largest part of our recent immigrants. The committee hopes all of us remember that, except for Native Americans, we are all immigrants.

SHARED-DECISION-MAKING COMMITTEE

A full discussion about major school events should be on the agenda of the shared-decision-making committee. Staff members would probably appreciate the timing of these activities since they do not interfere with the instructional priority and the pressures of beginning the second semester. Since it was their recommendation to have limited school-wide functions in December and January, the minutes should reflect the follow-up on their input.

Some discussion should be held on how the survey material could be used and how classes would select their team names. Issues include the following:

1. Which grade levels should be first in selecting their country's name?
2. What procedure will be used if two classes choose the same country?
3. Should priority be given to grades that are learning about the countries in their regular curriculum?
4. Is there agreement that the selection process should be done in February?
5. Will this be done by grade levels, at an assembly, or by submitting choices to the principal or a designee?

The decisions should be forwarded to all other schoolwide committees, announced at the faculty meeting, and shared with the PTA. The principal should include the information in the weekly memorandum or in the committee's minutes to ensure that all staff members are informed. An imperative of leadership is no surprises for the people on the front lines.

SCHOOL-COMMUNITY COMMITTEE

Educating the nonteaching members of the school-community committee about the need to have the professional staff reestablish an orderly
learning environment is the principal's obligation. After that is accomplished, there should be an open discussion about how these community members can assist with the olympics. Educators should never
underestimate potential input from parents and businesspersons.

The members of several service organizations in a suburb of Phila-
delphia developed a project that would have enhanced the olympic
events being planned by their school district. They read a story about a
project funded by Steven Spielberg to videotape Holocaust survivors
describing their experiences to have a permanent record of them. The
members of the local Lions' Club suggested that students interview
their oldest relatives and discover why they came to America. Since the
most recent wave of immigration was from the Hispanic community,
they believed it would be simple to tape their parents and grandparents,
most of whom live locally. The children whose families came from
Europe and Asia could do the same but might have to interview them
via e-mail, over the phone, or at family gatherings if they lived farther
away.

Rotary and chamber of commerce members might agree to bind several books of these stories and donate them to the school district's
libraries. When the principal presents ideas such as these at the faculty
meetings, the staff often becomes enthusiastic since it provides them
with additional motivation for their students. Once again, community
committee members may provide the ideas and the funding to make
the olympics a truly school-community event.

The principal would be wise to involve local residents in the judging
of several of the activities. There is a need to decide which essays to
use and which songs and dances to select to represent each grade level
at the spring concert, and official starters, judges, and scorekeepers are
needed at the final olympic-day competitions. Residents could assist at
judging.

PTA MEETING

The programs and activities being planned during the committee meetings would probably be known to the leaders of the PTA. Often these

activists are on several other committees and frequently touch base with the principal to learn about what's happening in the school. However, the dissemination of the plans to the PTA's general membership is essential. Members' involvement is actively sought since their input will enhance the quality of each activity. Parents are a helpful source of free publicity and provide additional supervision. At this meeting, the principal has an opportunity to explain the timing of the program. Parents also learn about how these activities are related to grade-level curriculum objectives.

Parents assist better when they know all the details. They also have positive feelings when the principal shares the entire planning process. In this scenario, we'd recommend the principal do the following:

1. Give the particulars for each event.
2. Discuss the reasons for the timelines and stress how important it is to maintain an orderly school environment.
3. Inform them about the school-community project and ask for volunteers to tell their families' reasons for coming to America.
4. Request volunteers to assist with judging and supervision.
5. Urge that members of the PTA help to publicize the events in the community and attend themselves.

Since we desire community involvement, a letter should be written to the students' parents and a copy sent to our residents and service organizations. One class's or the PTA's volunteering to draw posters to be placed in local business establishments would enhance the event's publicity.

North Gables Elementary School
555 Main Street
Gables, Texas 12345
Jane Carter
Principal
Re Upcoming Events

Dear Parents,

At the end of January, we will be completing the first half of our school year. As soon as the students return from the winter recess, our teachers will begin preparing them for the end of the month midterm examinations. I'm pleased to inform you that the educational tone of the building is excellent and both the children and the staff are maximizing their instructional time.

We also are planning a series of activities in which we hope to involve our entire community. As a follow-up to our successful Hispanic-international day, we wish to continue the warm feeling of togetherness the event generated. The staff, PTA, community committees, and service organizations have been involved in developing several programs during the last 2 months. Please note the following dates since we sincerely want you to attend all of our school functions:

- On Friday, March 27, each grade level will have a contest to decide which class will participate in the spring concert. The concert will include songs and dances from the country the class will represent in the olympics. Parents who speak a foreign language may be called upon by their children to help the class learn a song or to teach the students an original dance from their native land.
- On Friday, April 23, we will host the spring concert. During the evening, one class from each grade level will sing a song or perform a dance from the country the students will represent in the olympics. Our chorus, orchestra, and band will perform and accompany each class.
- On Friday, June 11, we will hold the year's culminating activity, the international olympics. Each class will have its country judged on the entrance parade, costumes, cheers, and participation in athletic contests. We invite parents to volunteer to assist us with supervision and judging each contest.

We want parents to know that these events will be coordinated with the history, geography, and current events the children are learning in their classes. We believe that each child's education will be enhanced by these carefully planned extracurricular programs.

Please join us for these events.

Sincerely,
Ms. Jane Carter, Principal

February: Solidifying School-Community Support and Participation in Upcoming Activities

Decisions determine destiny.

—Frederick Speakman

The principal should make the wishes of the faculty clear to all segments of the community. The faculty needed December and January to concentrate on academic material and to ensure that the major events for the school year were well planned. The timing was equally critical, and it allowed teachers to integrate subject matter material into segments of the olympic activities. The principal's objective is to harness the energy of school-community organizations until it is time to allow them to properly focus on the forthcoming decisions about the olympics. The process should capture the essence of shared decision making.

Armed with many suggestions, the principal should organize the kick off of the event. Early in February a schoolwide assembly would be held and one student from each class selected to pick a number from a hat to determine the order in which the team's country name would be selected. The students, we hope, would react enthusiastically to the number chosen by their classmate. Once this was completed, another student could draw the name of one of the members of the United Nations from the top of a huge world globe. After the country's name is chosen, the class has the right to accept it or reject it. If the students wanted a second chance, the class would have to wait until all other classes made their selection.

An exciting assembly and the enthusiasm engendered by the selection process should provide additional motivation for the program. Two days prior to the assembly, the principal should send another memorandum to each classroom teacher to follow up on the information about the names of every United Nations member. This would include the countries of origin for the families of the school's children. New data could be taken in part from a calendar that was the product of the Greater Boston Civil Rights Coalition and the Anti-Defamation League. The principal could share the January listing of holiday events for the nations and religions around the world, the purpose being to add to the olympic competition by having each class do the following:

1. Research a national holiday for the country it has chosen and record the date.
2. Determine a name of the country's national hero or first ruler.
3. Discover the major religious holiday for the country's population.
4. Have all of the preceding items placed on a monthly calendar that would be located in the school's library.

Each class would receive a score based upon the accuracy and promptness of the return of its research to the school's librarian. Although the principal provided the January international calendar, the February through December dates would be provided by the individual classes in the school. When the project is completed, a large calendar for each month could be displayed at the school's entrance and in the library. The principal would forward the information to the superintendent's office with the recommendation that all of the dates be placed on the district's school calendar for the following year.

This entire process should enable students do some elementary research. In the upper grades, the children would be able to go to the school or community library to obtain the required data. In the lower grades, teachers and parents could assist the children in the discovery of the information. Some of the teachers would probably expand the project by having their students write to their country's mission at the United Nations. The foreign delegations normally respond with posters, historical data, lists of famous heroes, and significant historical events. The children will learn about world geography, their nation's history, and letter-writing skills. These exercises should serve to enrich the project's curriculum component. Table 10.1 shows an example for January's entries.

The principal's duties go beyond the launching of the olympic activities. February is the start of the second semester. The principal should be doing the following:

1. Reviewing each teacher's grades.
2. Working on the following year's master schedule.
3. Informing the staff of the outcome of budget hearings with central-office administrators.
4. Planning summer curriculum-writing projects.
5. Checking on the status of school supplies.
6. Completing the evaluations of all nontenure staff members.

These responsibilities do not include the day-to-day activities necessary for administering the school's educational program and ensuring a businesslike academic tone. It is not an exaggeration to say that the principal rarely is able to complete the daily to-do list that constitutes his or her action agenda. Let's examine the monthly committee meetings in which the principal additionally must provide enthusiasm and leadership.

PTA EXECUTIVE-BOARD MEETING AND GENERAL MEETING

Noneducators are not aware that the principal usually attends two PTA meetings each month. The executive-board meeting is with the PTA officers, and the group plans the meetings and each member's responsibility to ensure its success. The second is the general meeting that is open to all members of the community. Its desired outcome is for the session to be meaningful and enjoyable. Generally the proactive principal will inform the PTA leaders about the school's activities, issues, and achievements. The leader will also make a presentation at the general meeting and to contribute toward its value and success.

In this scenario, the principal should fully describe the programs that

Table 10.1   Resource for Olympic Programs

January 1	New Year's Day
	St. Basil, Greek Orthodox
	National holiday, Cuba, Haiti, Sudan
	Paradura del Nino, Venezuela
	International Literacy Year
	IMANI (Faith) last day of Kwanzaa
	Independence Day, Haiti and Sudan
January 3	Guru Gobind Singh's birthday, Sikh
January 4	National holiday, Union of Burma
January 5	National holiday, Kiribati
	Twelfth Night, Christian
January 6	Epiphany, Catholic, Greek
January 7	Epiphany (in some countries)
	Ganna (Christmas), Ethiopia
	Christmas, Russian Orthodox
January 11	Hosto's birthday, Puerto Rico
January 12	Ati-Atihan, Philippines
January 13	National holiday, Togo
	Lohri, Hindu
January 14	New Year, Russian Orthodox
	Makara Sankranti, Hindu
January 15	Martin Luther King Day, United States
	Dia del Maestro, Venezuela
	Seijin No Hi, Japan
	Arbor Day, Jordan
January 17	St. Anthony's Day, Christian
January 19	Theophany, Russian Orthodox
	Timkat, Ethiopia
	Kitchen God, China
January 20	Babin Den, Bulgaria
January 24	Alasitas, Bolivia
January 25	Robert Burns Night, Scotland
January 26	National holiday, Australia and India
January 27	St. Devote, Monaco
	New Year, China, Korea
	Tet, Vietnam
January 31	National holiday, Nadru
	Basant Panchami, Hindu

will be the major events for the remainder of the school year and receive the help of PTA volunteers to assist with judging, security, and supervision. The parent organization should be a partner in the events, since it was involved in the initial determination of each of the school's programs. We would expect that parents would fulfill many active roles in the olympics.

They should do all of the following:

1. Assist with the selection process for team names.
2. Seek residents to tell or write their reasons for coming to America.
3. Judge several elements of the poster contests, dance performances, ethnic songs, and class costumes.
4. Assist teachers with the supervision of children at the concert and during the athletic events.
5. Publicize all of the programs.
6. Create posters for display in local business establishments to advertise the school activities.
7. Offer assistance to primary-grade teachers with students' makeup and costumes.
8. Communicate to the PTA membership the humanistic and educational value of the programs.

SCHOOL-COMMUNITY COMMITTEES

There is an educational responsibility that the principal should fulfill when dealing with the members of the school-community committee. Holding a premeeting with the community liaison will secure a valuable assistant for this task. The olympic activities should be viewed as the school's attempt to bring the community together. People leaving the meeting should feel that the committee leaders are doing everything in their power to open the doors for new residents to enjoy the right of equal participation in school-community festivities.

Having residents volunteer to take the dates and plans for the programs back to their own constituency is extremely valuable. Their endorsement is more effective than any written advertisements. Sometimes hearing the principal's message from their own representatives speaking in their own language makes it more credible. Their own networking often allows them to attend with families they know and trust. With this support system, the more timid individuals will have the courage to participate. This type of sensitivity rarely appears in a principal's job description.

SHARED-DECISION-MAKING COMMITTEE

The planning of the spring concert and the olympics should have been discussed at prior meetings of the shared-decision-making committee. Timelines that the faculty members recommend are usually consistent with their job responsibilities. They will avoid periods when their colleagues are under pressure or forced to meet other deadlines. The goal should be to gain the full endorsement of the staff since leaders should be aware that tacit approval usually secures uninspired participation. Ideally, we would recommend that a teacher member from this committee report the content of these discussions to the faculty at their monthly meeting.

In colder climates many school districts have elected to close for a winter vacation. The process began during the height of the nation's fuel crises but continues today. The week usually coincides with the celebration of Presidents' Day. The holiday is celebrated on Monday and the schools remain closed for the entire week. As a result, February can comprise as few as 15–17 school days. Spacing the events as we've recommended will allow the staff to have the full month of March and half of April to prepare for the spring concert and dance festival.

North Gables Elementary School
555 Main Street
Gables, Texas 12345
Jane Carter
Principal
Re Report Cards

Dear Parent,

Your child's second report card accompanies this letter. With half of the school year completed, we have a good indication of how your child is performing in class. Please read the entire report card and pay close attention to the teacher's comments about your child's behavior and effort in school. Frequently these items are the reasons the student receives excellent or poor grades. Effective homework preparation, attentiveness in class, outstanding effort, and good behavior are the characteristics of a high-performing student. The entire staff recommends that you take the time to talk with your child about his or her effort and attitude.

After reviewing the report card and discussing the results with your child, please sign the back of the report to indicate that you have received this vital communication, and return it to your child's teacher. If you have any comment, feel free to write your remarks in the designated section. Please be assured that every written comment will be read by your child's teacher. If the teacher feels a conference is necessary, we will call and arrange for the meeting. If for any reason you would like to discuss the report card, please call my office at 123–4567, and we will have the teacher contact you promptly. If you feel you would prefer to meet personally with your child's teacher, simply let my secretary know, and she will arrange a convenient time for the meeting.

We want to remind you about several events on our school calendar that you are invited to attend. We look forward to your participation since these activities will involve the entire school and our community.

SPRING CONCERT

Friday, April 23, at 7:30 p.m.

This year one class from each grade level will perform songs or dances from the country it will represent in our olympics in June. The classes chosen to perform in the program have already won a previous contest with every other class on their grade level. Members of our staff and PTA served as judges for these activities. Please attend this multicultural event, which will bring pride to our school and community.

Friday, June 11, 9 a.m.–3 p.m. (rain date, June 14)

In addition to the traditional athletic contests, our olympics will include an entrance parade, judging of native costumes, and cheering contests. We believe it is a fitting culmination to this year's attempt to honor all of our residents and their cultural heritage. Your participation in the event is the only thing necessary to make the program a greater success.

Sincerely,
Ms. Jane Carter, Principal

CHAPTER 11

March: Promoting Understanding and Motivation Through Staff In-Service Courses

A wise man will make more opportunities than he finds.

—Francis Bacon

March usually has approximately 21 to 23 days of school unencumbered by national or religious holidays. In April, there is a spring recess; in May, the Memorial Day celebration; and in June, examination week and the end of the school year. March is obviously a month of intense instruction. The principal has the added burden of balancing a workload that includes the urgent items listed in the following and the culminating plans for the school community:

1. Begin the kindergarten or pre-K screening process.
2. Prepare to defend budget recommendations for the following year.
3. Complete evaluations of all nontenure teachers.
4. Prepare staff for third-quarter report cards, usually issued in April.
5. Begin work on next year's master schedule.
6. Finalize recommendations for summer-curriculum projects.
7. Complete summer school bulletin describing course offerings.
8. Coordinate middle school orientation process for fifth graders.
9. Initiate new-teacher hiring process with central-office staff.
10. Finalize plans for the spring concert and the song and dance festival.

For our purposes, we will explore only item 10. The principal should present guidelines for the competition to decide which class will represent the grade at the spring concert and dance festival. Suggesting that PTA officers or administrators be given the responsibility to judge the contest will avoid possible conflicts between classroom teachers. Urging that the process be conducted early in the month will allow the winning class to have a few weeks to practice prior to the event.

The principal should offer some guidance about the nation each class would select. The teacher and class should consider several aspects of the country's values to be able to replicate their songs, dances, and cultures. The parents from foreign nations, whose children attend the school, would be a valuable resource for the teacher and class. They would probably be able to lend them articles of their traditional dress, contribute pictures and artifacts for displays, and perhaps even offer to teach traditional dances. They certainly would help in the identification of famous people who emigrated from their native land.

In a Florida school district, one class requested permission to have a famous Hispanic entertainer accompany them during the spring concert. The students had written letters to nine famous people who had Cuban roots and requested them to attend the performance. On their list were not only entertainers but also politicians from Florida and major league baseball stars. This was a valuable research component to the event and fostered the skill of writing business letters. Even though few of the celebrities attended, the children treasured the autographed letters and pictures they received in response to their letters of invitation.

There is an educational debate that has continued over the past few decades about how foreign-born children should be taught English and when they should be integrated into regular classes. Unfortunately, the debate has taken on noneducational arguments, specifically, those in the political and economic arenas. We highly recommend that principals provide in-service training in this matter to both new and experienced faculty members. We would suggest that in addition to the weekly memorandum, an issues-related research paper be sent to each school's staff. In one Connecticut school district, a shared-decision-making committee sends written updates in October, January, March, and May. Here is a typical newsletter to staff.

Newsletter

As a faculty we had limited input into the board of education's decision about how our foreign-born students or, more precisely, how our children who speak English as a second language would be taught. It is each board of education's prerogative and legal responsibility to decide which academic programs will be taught. Their action is taken after considering the recommendations of the superintendent of schools. We are not quarreling with the decision but want the faculty to be fully aware of the theoretical issues that were explored by our central-office staff prior to the board's decision.

How to teach foreign-language-speaking students English has always been a controversial issue. The methodology has serious implications for teachers and learners. Many older Americans feel that their parents learned English without any special program. They were thrust into regular classrooms with teachers who often could not speak their language, and yet they learned enough language skills for them to get along in school and the labor force. Full exposure to speaking English is also advocated by financially minded citizens who want to reduce spending on programs that they consider unnecessary. For some who resent the influx of recent immigrants, proactive programs such as bilingual education or instruction in English as a second language are viewed as being politically incorrect. As educators we have the responsibility to constantly search to improve our instructional methodology. We are aware of those who oppose any programs to improve language instruction for our foreign-language-speaking students but we agree to disagree.

Let's examine the differences between bilingual education and an ESL program. As educators we should be conversant with each method to be able to discuss the issues intelligently and to make our own professional judgments. We should be able to appraise both instructional philosophies without making decisions predicated on political or economic considerations.

For those who wonder why this continues to be of importance to American educators, we remind you of the following:

1. There are presently almost 3 million limited-English-proficient (LEP) children in our school systems.

2. Believe it or not, more than 50% of these students were born in the United States!
3. Spanish-speaking children make up more than 2.2 million of our LEP population.
4. As we noted before, schools in all of the large urban areas of the United States have children who speak dozens of foreign languages. How we as educators advocate instructing these young people is our profession's responsibility.

BILINGUAL EDUCATION

The primary premise of bilingual education is that the child should first fully develop skills in his or her own language. After accomplishing this vital task, the pupil can become proficient in English. Most of us on the committee reminded the bilingual advocates that many of our children have never attended school in their native country when they arrive in America. We therefore questioned the basic premise.

The bilingual education process, according to educational researchers, takes 5 to 7 years to achieve fluency in English. They believe that the child should be taught to read in his or her native tongue before being taught to read English. Our staff made several additional points that questioned the basic premise of bilingual education. We reminded the advocate that we don't have teachers who are fluent in the language of many of our new immigrants. We could probably instruct children in Spanish but are unable to teach any of the Asian languages or Russian. Also, our experience has shown that the quicker a student is immersed in hearing and speaking English, the faster the pace of learning. Clearly, our reaction to the use of bilingual education came into question.

Many researchers have concluded that there is little or no benefit from native-language teaching. Their study results have suggested that the bilingual education process does not speed the learning of English nor does it help in the mastering of other academic courses. In short, educators now believe that limited-

English-speaking students learn better when English is the language of instruction. We have bilingual students but no longer recommend the bilingual instructional methodology.

ENGLISH AS A SECOND LANGUAGE

The terms *bilingual education* and *English as a second language* are often used interchangeably. They are clearly different instructional methods. We've defined bilingual education and discussed several reasons why it is no longer in favor. Both programs were intended to teach proficiency in English but were distinguished by different instructional strategies. Unlike bilingual education, the ESL program attempts to rely almost exclusively on the use of English. ESL proponents strongly believe that children will more rapidly learn basic language skills and thus be integrated into regular academic classes in a relatively short time.

Our shared-decision-making committee supports the superintendent's recommendation and the board of education's decision to use the ESL program to educate our limited-English-speaking students. We hope this newsletter reminds our faculty members that we all should continue our efforts to develop a better understanding of these children. Many of the programs we've jointly sponsored with the PTA and school-community committee have been the means by which we chose to address the needs and problems of our non-English-speaking children. We applaud your professional efforts and the creative participation of your classes. Finally, we recommend several in-service courses to help us learn additional techniques to use English in the instruction of our limited-English-speaking population.

The 10th responsibility of the principal listed at the beginning of this chapter needs additional consideration. The principal should design a list of due dates accompanied by the name of the each person responsible for their completion for both the April spring concert and the June olympic games similar to table 11.1.

The to-do list of responsibilities for the culminating olympics in June should be itemized in May. The thoroughness of this schedule is

Table 11.1 April Spring Concert

Activity	Person Responsible	Date Completed
1. Selection of team names	Principal	February 27
2. Review songs	Principal	March 5
3. Meet with music staff	Principal	March 15
4. Set up for assembly	Assistant principal	March 21
5. Supervision (day)	Principal	March 21
6. Supervision (night)	Assistant principal	April—TBA
7. Invitations (parents)	Principal	April—TBA
8. Invitations (residents)	Principal	April—TBA
9. Written program	Assistant principal	April—TBA
10. Preview dances	Principal	April—TBA
11. Assembly seating chart	Assistant principal	April—TBA
12. Preview displays	Principal	April—TBA
13. Check public address system	Head custodian	April—TBA
14. Arrange rehearsal schedule	Assistant principal	April—TBA
15. Call police concerning parking	School secretary	April—TBA

Note: TBA = to be announced.

stressed since it's vitally important for the school year to end on a positive note. The principal and staff must be focused on planning and structuring the event to maximize educational outcomes and to end the school year with students feeling a sense of pride and enthusiasm. It is an enormous motivational, organizational, and educational challenge for the school's principal.

North Gables Elementary School
555 Main Street
Gables, Texas 12345
Jane Carter
Principal
Re Information Update

Dear Parents,

Next month we are planning our annual spring concert. This year we are celebrating the diversity of our community by having classes perform the songs and dances of many foreign countries. This will be a lead-up activity for our June olympics.

Each class has chosen a country to represent at the concert. We would like to invite everyone who resides in the school district to attend the assembly program. The staff is also requesting some assistance from your family to help make the songs, dances, and costumes more authentic. We have listed below each class and the country it will represent at the concert. If you or any member of your family would like to volunteer to help the class that selected your nation of birth, we would appreciate your participation in the project. We invite you to speak to the class, lend us examples of your ethnic dress, or help demonstrate the songs and dances of your heritage. If you phone the school at 123–4567, the classroom teacher will return your call and set up a mutually agreeable time to meet.

Class	Country	Teacher
K-100	Korea	Ms. Jones
K-101	Spain	Mrs. Hart
K-103	Cuba	Ms. Foster
1-104	Russia	Ms. Spencer
1-105	Puerto Rico	Mrs. West
1-106	Poland	Mrs. Gavin
2-107	Vietnam	Ms. Marvin
2-108	France	Ms. Martinez
2-109	Ireland	Mrs. Homer
3-110	Germany	Mrs. Young
3-111	Iran	Mr. Giles
3-200	India	Mrs. Carmen
4-201	Pakistan	Mr. Roth
4-202	Mexico	Mr. Fitz
4-203	Japan	Ms. Grant
5-204	Portugal	Mr. Brown
5-205	China	Mr. Schultz
5-206	Ghana	Mr. Harding

Please call if you wish to become involved. It does not have to be your child's class. Also add the following dates to your calendar:

Spring concert, Friday, April 23, at 7:30 p.m.
International olympics, Friday, June 11, at 9:00 a.m.

Sincerely,
Ms. Jane Carter, Principal

CHAPTER 12

April: Exploring Long-Range Commitments and Planning Culminating Events

A principal is a VIP. He or she has Vision, Integrity, and Passion.

—George Melton

During the middle of April, the third quarter of the academic year is completed. Along with report cards, it is necessary to write letters to parents whose children are performing inadequately. This is imperative information for parents since it affords them the opportunity to help their children with closer supervision of homework and to hire tutors to prepare them for standardized tests and final examinations. In the primary grades, teacher-parent conferences usually take the place of these formal letters. The principal has several districtwide responsibilities that must be addressed prior to June. These activities include major functions drawn from the school leader's job description. The principal should be doing the following:

1. Finalizing the building's budget and preparing for its defense at a superintendent's hearing.
2. Completing all nontenure-staff evaluations and informing central-office personnel whether teachers are to be rehired and, if not, posting the positions.
3. Preparing the examination schedule for mandated achievement tests or teacher-developed grade-level examinations.
4. Orienting fifth-grade students and their parents concerning the middle school program with the cooperation of guidance counselors and other middle school administrators.

5. Interviewing candidates for projected staff openings.
6. Completing the master schedule for the upcoming year.
7. Planning the year-end moving-up exercise.
8. Updating the PTA about the year-end calendar, the spring concert, and the June olympics.
9. Informing the school-community committee of the status of the spring concert and the olympics.
10. Scheduling all preparation, rehearsals, decorations, supervisory responsibilities, and timelines for the spring concert.

The principal's weekly memorandum to staff should also provide in-service information. Under the heading of research data, the school's leader has an opportunity to make the staff aware of current trends affecting education. Some faculty members may be reluctant to adjust their teaching to respond to recent immigration patterns. Often these teachers believe their district is the only one confronting the huge influx of bilingual students. Information such as presented in table 12.1 can easily be obtained from the National Center for Educational Statistics.

This information should be provided to the residents via the school-

Table 12.1   Research Data (States With 50,000 or More Hispanic Students)

State	Hispanic Population	% of Total Population
Arizona	280,000	33
California	2,500,000	42
Colorado	147,500	21
Connecticut	71,000	13
Florida	433,000	18
Georgia	57,000	4
Illinois	296,000	14
Massachusetts	99,000	10
Michigan	55,000	3
Nevada	78,000	24
New Jersey	192,000	15
New Mexico	160,000	50
New York	528,000	18
Oregon	52,000	9
Pennsylvania	77,000	4
Texas	1,579,000	40
Washington	96,000	10

Source: National Conference of States Legislatures, n.d.

community committee. This data assists all school constituents in understanding that we are in the midst of a new immigration phenomena, and the school's curriculum and the staff's instructional methodology must make adjustments to remain effective.

PTA MEETING

Parental cooperation is needed for the spring concert. Committees should be formed to help with publicity and decorations. A discussion about whether refreshments will be served after the program should be held. The principal's guidance is necessary since if it is a long program, refreshments should not be planned. It is unwise to extend the evening for this age group.

Parents must also be thoroughly informed about the culminating activities planned for June. The principal should discuss with parents the educational value of all planned events and programs. Emphasis should be on the research required of each class and the involvement of community members in the preparation of songs and dance routines. Although there will be awards for the winners of athletic contests, the members of the PTA should be invited to serve as judges for the entrance parade, costumes, cheers, and sportsmanlike behavior.

Discussing the moving-up exercise and the testing schedules is recommended. If the summer school program has been finalized, the principal may wish to review its course offerings. This type of presentation informs key parents about forthcoming activities and allows them to share the information with their general membership.

SCHOOL-COMMUNITY COMMITTEE

The school-community committee should be involved in the planning of both the spring concert and the June olympics. Residents could loan classes costumes and artifacts of their culture. Some parents may even demonstrate dances indigenous to the land of their birth.

Service organizations often donate items that enhance the appearance of the program. In one Atlanta suburb, the chamber of commerce purchased baseball hats with the interlocking-circle insignia of the

International Olympic Committee for use by all judges and officials. In Hartford, Connecticut, a service club secured an Olympic flag from a local vendor to display, while on Long Island an Italian American club lent a large flag to the team representing Italy.

Initial discussions should be held about possible follow-up programs for the next school year. Committee members could be given a homework problem to consider. They could be asked to generate a list of similar programs they've heard or read about that could maintain or improve upon the accomplishments achieved this year.

SHARED-DECISION-MAKING COMMITTEE

With the year's events planned, the shared-decision-making committee should turn its attention to future challenges. Its members should engage in a similar follow-up assignment to that given to the school-community committee. How does the staff build upon the multicultural emphasis of this year and design new initiatives with meaningful instructional objectives?

A committee that functions with a true understanding of the shared-decision-making process would probably seek ways to receive input from the entire staff. One excellent strategy to involve teachers is to develop a survey instrument of possible school enrichment activities. Committee members could review current research and poll other districts to learn what multicultural events they have found to be most effective. The survey instrument shown here was used by the shared-decision-making middle school team in Mineola, New York.

Survey

To: All Staff

From: The Members of the Shared-Decision-Making Team

Topic: Staff Input for Next Year's Major Academic Functions

Your committee has taken several weeks to make contact with many other districts in an attempt to learn about their successful multicultural activities. We are pleased that our colleagues in other school communities have sent us their recommendations that are delineated below.

We have also surveyed several authors who write on the topics of multi-cultural education and diversity and added their ideas to our list. Perhaps most important of all, we have provided space for your ideas since we believe that you more than anyone know the territory.

SUCCESSFUL PROGRAM RECOMMENDATION

1. Create a multicultural library to house teacher materials, videos, and books on diverse cultures.
2. Have every grade level list the ways they teach appreciation for other ethnic groups.
3. Establish a multicultural club or diversity club that corresponds with similar organizations in the state and nation.
4. Generate a monthly multicultural newspaper to describe community events, ethnic heroes, and humanistic stories about family struggles to reach America.
5. Encourage projects to augment the school's library materials by developing bibliographies, displays, audiovisual materials, and collections of family artifacts.
6. Host an international food festival.
7. Conduct a multicultural fair or festival.
8. Develop a list of community members who would host an annual teach-in for each grade level.
9. Construct monthly bulletin boards to honor different cultures.
10. Have a hall of fame representing famous Americans from different ethnic and religious groups who have contributed to our society.
11. Have each class establish pen pals with students throughout the country (world), and develop a book of interesting letters for the school library.
12. Organize an essay contest on the evils of prejudice. Have winning entries read during an assembly.
13. Have a poster contest on the theme of responding to bias incidents.
14. Have a poetry contest on the theme of respecting other cultures. Publish the winning poems in book form and place in the school library or multicultural center.

15. Create a speakers bureau of students who will talk about their heritage to students, residents, and community groups.

Please add any of your own ideas. Return by next Friday. We will discuss the results at our next shared-decision-making meeting in May.

_____

_____

_____

_____

_____

_____

SPRING CONCERT NEWS

The spring concert was held during April. The event provided the entire school-community with a program that fostered a feeling of mutual respect and exceptional educational activities. In the process in which each class selected a country to represent at the concert, students made their decision based upon a multitude of factors. They used the library to determine the exact location of the country, its physical shape, and its national flag. They examined the list of foreign countries whose children attend their school. They examined data about their national heroes. Then each class held discussions about whether the country had an exciting song or a spirited national dance. This provided an excellent example of using research information prior to making a decision.

After rehearsing their songs or dances, each class was part of a grade-level competition. The winning class represented its grade in the spring contest. Those who lost began preparing their songs, costumes, and entrance parade for the June olympics. Teachers used both losing and winning as additional motivation.

The concert provided the school with a platform to demonstrate their students' talent. The invited audience included parents, grandparents, residents, business owners, and civic officials. Entering an auditorium featuring the flags of all nations and student-designed poster displays made the experience more festive for all in attendance.

North Gables Elementary School
555 Main Street
Gables, Texas 12345
Jane Carter
Principal
Re Thank You

Dear Parents,

Our staff wanted me to thank our parents for their exceptional support during the planning of the spring concert. The enthusiastic response by parents and community residents to the live performance was greatly appreciated by the children and their teachers. We fulfilled our goal to develop an activity for the school and community that would be unifying in spirit and educationally sound. I wanted you all to know how proud I am of our entire staff for their hard work and enthusiastic support for the project.

Your child's report card is accompanying this letter. Please remember that we are entering the final quarter of our school year. In the event that you have any question about a grade or conduct mark, please call and we'll arrange an appointment with your child's teacher. Our school's phone number is 123–4567. We feel some urgency in hearing any of your concerns at this time because it is the only way to avoid disappointments at the end of the year. When in doubt, please call!

During May, our teachers will be concentrating on preparing your children for state achievement tests and other local examinations. During this month, we have not planned any major functions or field trips for the children to maximize our instructional time. We ask parents to help by checking their children's homework and making sure they attend school prepared for their day's work.

Toward the end of June, the staff has planned a wholesome culminating activity for your children. It will be a follow-up to our recent spring concert. The event will be an international olympics. Classes will compete in an entrance parade, cheering, and costume contests. Each class will represent a foreign nation. Children will also be involved in athletic contests and team sports. Save the date June 22, 9:30 a.m., on your calendar. If you have the time to assist us as judges or safety supervisors, please call the main office.

Up to now we have had an extremely positive and productive school year. Our seriousness of purpose during the month of May is to ensure that we will reach all of our academic goals. Remember, we are here to be partners with you in your child's education. Your suggestions are encouraged, and your involvement in our school's activities is always appreciated.

Sincerely,
Ms. Jane Carter, Principal

CHAPTER 13

May: Acknowledging and Justifying School and Community Participation

To accomplish great things, we must not only act, but also dream; not only plan, but believe.

—Anatole France

May is the academic homestretch. The budget is now in the hands of the public. The building's budgetary needs have been stated and defended before the superintendent and board of education. The issues raised by the third-quarter report cards have been addressed by the staff in meetings with parents. The principal's plan to stress grade-level subject matter should now be effectively implemented by the faculty. Several other tasks remain prior to confronting June's culminating activities. These responsibilities include all of the following:

1. Finalize the summer school program.
2. Complete all teacher evaluations.
3. Hold final committee meetings and establish goals for the upcoming year.
4. Initiate school-closing procedures.
5. Oversee the administration of standardized examinations.
6. Host final PTA meeting.
7. Conduct all remaining fire drills.
8. Plan for the supervision of graduation and the olympics.
9. Order and sign student diplomas.
10. Distribute final progress reports.
11. Continue hiring process for new staff members.
12. Meet with custodial staff to plan summer maintenance projects.

13. Submit list of cocurricular advisors for next year.
14. Coordinate the schedule of school pictures.

While working on all of the tasks we've listed, how does the school's leader maintain and possibly accentuate the warm afterglow of the spring concert experience? Certainly the principal has complimented the staff and student body in various ways. Expressing gratitude over the public address system the day after the concert is just the beginning. A letter to parents written by the principal should include high praise for the staff. Additionally, the principal should post on the teachers' bulletin board the many grateful notes received from members of the community, the superintendent, and local business organizations. Finally, individual notes of appreciation to staff members for their extraordinary efforts should be written and become a part of their professional file.

It is valuable to regenerate enthusiasm for this type of activity and for the culminating olympics scheduled for June. Sharing current data about how other schools are reaching out to their populations of limited-English-speaking students and parents is a helpful technique. We've stressed many of these schoolwide activities in a previous chapter. There is also a wealth of material in professional journals and even more current data in newspapers and magazines.

A national newspaper provides snapshots of how schools across the nation are responding to their new immigrant student populations. New York City has just announced the establishment of an academy that will help educators better teach those for whom English is a second language. It is an idea used in many smaller districts across the United States, and as you will see in our final chapter, most model programs will offer basic foreign-language instruction to their faculty and staff. One beneficial insight gained from this academy plan is that the curriculum will be collaboratively developed by university scholars and school leaders. School districts should have their in-service courses designed in a similar manner and allow teachers to receive course credit toward another college degree for their participation. Districts frequently offer credit for these courses that entitle staff members to move up on the salary scale.

Some thought-provoking articles that appeared in recent newspapers and magazines offer further evidence that educators have to continue to explore new methods to improve their instructional techniques for limited-English-speaking children and use proactive techniques to reach out to these new immigrant families. Although we concentrate on educational strategies, our staff should recognize that newly arrived immigrants have become major social and economic issues in contemporary political campaigns.

After passage of the North American Free Trade Agreement many U.S. companies relocated to Mexico. These companies are now moving to Asia where labor is even cheaper. The ramification for U.S. schools is a huge influx of Mexican laborers and their families. Schools located in the American Southwest are being inundated by documented and undocumented Mexican children. This has become not only a political issue but an international crisis.

American labor unions have made an issue of the recent immigration patterns. The political and economic consequences are sure to produce fallout for those of us in education. Legislators could reduce educational spending for limited-English-speaking programs or enact immigration laws that are more restrictive. Teachers should be made aware that we must not isolate ourselves in the world of academia.

A prestigious high school in Manhattan that once offered French, German, and Spanish has now added Mandarin, Hebrew, Italian, Japanese, Korean, and Latin to the curriculum. People in other areas of the country may be surprised that this school's latest recommended new course is Arabic. The Muslim Student Association requested the addition of the course. An analysis of the new language offerings in schools will allow social scientists to trace recent immigration trends. Staff members should note that the largest increase in religious membership has been in the Muslim faith. This has never occurred before in our nation's history.

In response to the presence of more than 2.2 million Hispanics in the New York City area, a preschool in Manhattan is teaching a dual-language program to 2-year-old children from English-speaking middle-class homes. It is common knowledge that foreign language can be more effectively taught if instruction begins in the primary grades. However, most school districts across the nation usually offer foreign-language courses for the first time in middle schools. The only explanation is that, up to now, it has been viewed as an additional financial burden. For those of us who know how hesitant immigrant parents are to mobilize and exert the necessary pressure to propose earlier implementation of foreign-language instruction, we understand why the issue has had few spokespersons. The appeal of foreign-language teachers to start instruction in earlier grades is often viewed as being self-serving, instead of legitimate advice from experts. It is interesting that a small private preschool has recognized that New York City children should know Spanish if they are to function in their social environment and in their future world of employment.

On the other hand, many communities across the nation have also been involved in attempting to pass English-only laws. This is obviously a multifaceted political issue that also has educational ramifications. The goal for those of us in the field of education is to teach our foreign-born students as much English as quickly as possible. The debate centers around how best to accomplish this objective. Teachers should monitor the English-only debate to ensure that the political proponents do not infringe upon our responsibility to determine how to best educate our foreign-born students.

Many articles have been written about foreigners who are day laborers. In local communities, residents are often upset that these immigrants congregate on street corners and wait for offers of work from local contractors or residents. Other citizens are critical of the fact that these men and women, frequently undocumented aliens, are taking jobs away from Americans. Many object to them moving into their community. This is a social and political issue and good people have divergent views on how to resolve the problem. As educators we have to obey state and national laws. In many states, principals are required to register any student, regardless of citizenship, if he or she resides within the community's boundaries. Registration requirements should be explained to the staff and the community. Our focus should be to develop and maintain a safe learning environment for our foreign-born children, no matter what our political leanings. We believe all children can learn and deserve an excellent education.

There has been a series of articles in the press and in professional journals that attempt to academically differentiate between racial and ethnic groups. Asians are often referred to as the good immigrants. To designate one immigrant population as being superior to another is a dangerous practice. Our challenge is to begin instruction at the child's readiness level. Frequently, waves of immigrants from the same foreign country are dramatically different. Teachers across the nation have reported that when foreign-born children have received an education in their own native country, they generally learn English more quickly. Conversely, the child who has never attended school in the nation of his or her birth is usually more educationally challenged. Principals should share articles and recent data with their staff as in-service training, but the educational focus remains, as ever, to meet the child's individual needs. Expectations should not be limited or raised because of a child's membership in one particular ethnic, racial, or religious group.

Another issue is the paucity of certified teachers who are themselves members of the Hispanic or other minority communities. In every newspaper's help-wanted ads there are recruiting fairs seeking culturally and ethnically diverse staff members. These teachers provide instant role models for the children. You may find our views surprising on this issue since we believe that the focus of the hiring process should be to secure the most competent probationary teacher. If all other factors are equal, we certainly recommend the hiring of the minority candidate. Otherwise, we prefer to select the candidate who finished first in the screening process.

A final caution is to avoid stereotyping the minority candidate. A principal reminded us that he was guilty of minimizing a staff member's competency because of her Spanish accent. Weeks after he hired her, he learned that the teacher had been an attorney in Ecuador, the land of her birth. After hearing the story another principal informed us that his school's social worker had been a medical doctor in Peru. These foreign-born teaching recruits often have had to make many career adjustments to economically survive in their new country. Ask staff members to assess whether they are initially biased toward those with foreign accents. It should be a personal challenge to overcome this attitude. The principal should recognize that moralizing doesn't work, but admitting that you personally struggled with such problems will often help staff members to confront their own biases.

We are aware of the numerous year-end responsibilities the principal must address in May. Although the tasks are daunting, this book's thesis espouses the constant responsibility of school leaders to remain pro-active in maximizing the educational opportunity for the limited-English-speaking community. Providing in-service education to staff members on current trends in the instruction of these children is also advantageous. These children rarely have another advocate, and thus we urge principals to become the conscience of their community and have this population's needs as part of their action agenda.

SHARED-DECISION-MAKING COMMITTEE

In April the shared-decision-making committee should write a memo-randum to the entire faculty in which it includes the results of the sur-vey taken about multicultural programs. The memo could list many activities that school districts had undertaken to enhance their caring environment and the goals of their limited-English-speaking program. The committee could attend the May faculty meeting, review the sur-vey, and elicit additional program ideas from the staff. After the discus-sion the faculty could recommend two programs for the following year. Both events should be consistent with the required curriculum and con-tinue the effort to bring the entire community together.

The staff may want to develop a multicultural library as was done in another district. However, they should plan to go beyond a mere collec-tion of books and materials. They could feature a different culture dur-ing the months of October through the month of May. Each class would be able to visit the display of artifacts and costumes and hear a story told by a person representing that culture. Follow-up activities would be done in individual classrooms and be consistent with that grade's curriculum goals.

The second activity would be some type of community fair or festi-val. The final decision of how each class would be involved would be left up to the shared-decision-making committee and the grade-level leaders. The event could also involve members of the community and local business and civic organizations.

MAY PTA MEETING

The PTA's meeting's agenda will be set by the officers of the PTA. The principal should request time to discuss the June olympics and establish PTA committees to help judge the events and to assist with the supervision of the children on the athletic field. The PTA could establish a three-person committee to judge the entrance parade and a second committee to judge the costumes of each team. Several individual members should volunteer to serve as starters and judges for the athletic contests. At the suggestion of the principal, a committee could be formed to select the class that exhibited the best sportsmanship during the competition. Finally, parents should volunteer to assist with the distribution of refreshments at the conclusion of the contest.

This meeting also affords the principal an opportunity to explain to parents the goals of the event. Although we want the children to have fun, our prime responsibility is to make certain that the program is a positive learning experience. Yes, principals also provide their students' parents with in-service instruction!

SCHOOL-COMMUNITY COMMITTEE

School-community committee members would be actively involved with the personnel on the shared-decision-making committee in conducting a survey and in the planning of event alternatives for the following year. Committee members might volunteer their assistance and several businesses in town could participate by making contributions of material and financial donations.

The committee also could conduct preliminary discussions about the goals for the following year. The committee could sponsor a community-wide event that would augment the school's planned major functions. The members could poll different communities to determine whether one of their programs would be worthy of replication. A list of these possibilities would provide the agenda for the June meeting, and the goal would be to get consensus on the recommended project.

North Gables Elementary School
555 Main Street
Gables, Texas 12345
Jane Carter
Principal
Re A Call for Suggestions from Parents

Dear Parents,

In the letter I wrote to you in April, I complimented the entire community for their wonderful comments about our spring concert. The event brought all of our residents together and the children performed admirably. We believe it promoted a positive community feeling and most felt that this type of school-community activity should become an annual happening.

The staff has requested that we invite everyone to offer suggestions for a follow-up program since they firmly believed it also had educational value. In a survey designed by our shared-decision-making committee, we received many suggestions from other communities and school districts. At the end of this letter, we have provided space for your recommendations. You may return the letter with your child and the staff will consider every suggestion at their next meeting. We strongly believe our parents are a vital part of the solution of every school challenge.

Please remember the schoolwide olympics that will take place next month on our own athletic field. Many parents and residents will be joining us since the program is a celebration of our residents' diverse cultures. Save the date June 22, 9:30 a.m., on your calendar.

The following are my suggestions for a major school-community event:

_____

_____

Signature (optional) _____

(Kindly return all suggestions to the main office.)

Sincerely,
Ms. Jane Carter, Principal

CHAPTER 14

June: Year-End Activities and Suggested Summer Reading Lists

Teaching is love made visible.

—Kahlil Gibran

The principal has to bring to closure many job responsibilities during the last month of the school year. Obviously, the two major culminating activities will be graduation and the major schoolwide event. In this case, the olympics is intended to bring together teachers and students in a memorable program that is meant to have a beneficial ripple effect throughout the community.

We would be remiss if we failed to specify the other major tasks that have to be addressed during the month. The school principal's assignments include the following:

1. Completing the promotion and retention list.
2. Monitoring the final report card process.
3. Finalizing all staff evaluations.
4. Collecting lists from teachers about their classroom's physical needs.
5. Attending final functions of the PTA, business organizations, faculty, and cultural clubs.
6. Submitting summer school plans and staffing.
7. Securing a list of staff members' summer addresses.
8. Meeting with the head custodian to determine summer work schedule.
9. Completing faculty interviews.
10. Organizing final teacher checkout procedures.

These responsibilities are often increased by requests from central-office personnel. The pressures are compounded by parental requests, invitations to attend community-wide functions, and state mandated requirements such as fire-drill-completion reports. In June setting priorities becomes a survival skill for every harried administrator.

We advocate the fostering of mutual respect as an educational priority. Developing a humanistic environment has a positive effect upon staff. This type of caring atmosphere establishes a supportive school environment for children. Violence and bullying rarely occur, and if they do, they are firmly handled by teachers and administrators. All forms of hateful behavior are simply not tolerated. This principle is nonnegotiable.

We will outline agendas for each of our standing committees in an attempt to present dual, simultaneous plans for closure for the current year and putting ideas in motion for the future. This is similar to the principal's organizing a calm end of the school year while being involved in the hiring of new staff members, refining the master schedule, and preparing summer work schedules for the custodial staff. Additionally, it affords the principal the opportunity to personally thank all committee members. Verbal acknowledgments should be accompanied by a letter for each deserving person's professional file.

- shared-decision-making committee
  - say thank you for a job well done
  - give additional praise for functioning like a model shared-decision-making committee
  - offer ways to assist the staff with ideas for next year's development of a multicultural library
  - determine whether the second community event be a fair or a festival
  - discuss event ideas
  - explore tentative dates for each event that will not interfere with instructional priorities
  - suggest ways the community should be involved in the proposed event
  - suggest ways committee members will be involved in the olympics
  - suggest future topics for the committee to investigate

- school-community committee
  - thank members for their support and participation
  - discuss members' roles in the olympics
  - announce faculty events for the following year
  - discuss how the committee will assist and get involved
  - accept suggestions for additional initiatives to assist members of the community
  - decide on your target population: foreign-born residents or the community at large
  - discuss securing new members for the committee
  - evaluate the work of the committee
- PTA meeting
  - thank everyone for their assistance throughout the school year
  - meet with new officers
  - discuss possible programs for the following year
  - discuss how the PTA can support the multicultural library and the community fair
  - establish PTA committees
  - inform PTA membership of principal's academic plans for the following year
  - conduct a question-and-answer period
  - plan an orientation program for new officers of the PTA
- adult-education committee
  - thank everyone for their time and suggestions
  - evaluate this year's programs and attendance by community members
  - accept suggestions for new programs
  - discuss how to develop a better brochure to announce adult programs
  - explore ways to support the school's community efforts
  - evaluate the bilingual parenting program

Principals are aware that endings require as much attention as beginnings. The remaining major events are the olympics and the graduation ceremony. Meticulous planning is required to make certain that these two culminating activities add to the positive image of the school's reputation. The schedule for the olympics delineates the responsibilities of school personnel, and it should be presented both at a faculty meeting and in writing to the entire staff.

Experienced principals usually augment their academic plans when developing schoolwide events with techniques to assure proper audience control. Structured procedures to enter the assembly, to control the audience throughout the activity, and to foster an orderly dismissal are vital to its success. The administrator's planning skills should be used from the beginning of the year to the final graduation ceremony.

Elementary school graduation ceremonies should not compete with the more prestigious event at the high school. This is a moving-up exercise and not a formal cap-and-gown affair. However, it remains an opportunity for the principal and staff to develop school traditions and to use the opportunity to enhance the school's public relations image. We would expect the school to exhibit to the community a goal of not only an outstanding academic program but also helping children become caring and responsible citizens. To that end, our graduation ceremony should honor students who have given service to the school or community with the same fervor that we usually reserve for our academic scholars. Those who worked on charity drives should also receive recognition. One of the ways we express our commitment to our limited-English-speaking children and their families is by having the student who wrote the most poignant essay on the theme read his or her work at graduation. Also having an encore presentation of one or two songs from the spring concert would be entertaining and should add dignity to the program. Finally, the theme of the graduation should be consistent with our other school-community activities. We are there not only to entertain but to educate.

Staff Memorandum
To: All Staff
From: Principal Jane Carter
Re: Olympics
Date: June 4

Teachers should submit names of students participating in the 60-yard dash and the marathon to the office by the end of school tomorrow.

Prior to the start of the olympics, teachers should remain with their classes until they are called to their position in the entrance parade via the PA system.

Judges will observe the parade and rate each class on its formation and its costumes.

Every teacher will be given a seating chart of the stadium in which the reserved section for the class will be noted.

We have added a sportsmanship award for the best-behaved class to assist teacher and parent supervisors with audience control.

Track events will be held by grade levels. There will be relays and a tug of war that will ensure the participation of every student. The other two events will be a 60-yard dash and a marathon. Please note that the marathon is simply a race in which the contestants will run two times around the track (about a half mile).

A lunch will be served to everyone courtesy of our parent-teacher association. Students will be invited up by class to avoid a disorderly rush to the serving stations. Please notify your classes that our youngest children will be served first.

An awards ceremony will follow lunch.

There will also be a recessional parade that will be judged as well. This is being done to assure an orderly end to the olympics.

Since we will still have about an hour left in the school day, we will have an essay and drawing contest with our olympic theme. Grades K–2 will draw a scene from the olympics and grades 3–5 will write an essay on a related theme such as sportsmanship, mutual respect, or ways to unite the people of the world. The winning composition will be read at our graduation ceremony.

I am aware of the hectic nature of this month and greatly appreciate your cooperation and professionalism. We have given our students an event to remember and cherish for years to come. This will be a fitting culmination to a wonderful school year.

North Gables Elementary School
555 Main Street
Gables, Texas 12345
Jane Carter
Principal
Re Event Update

Dear Parents,

The entire staff joins with me in giving our thanks to the parents of the North Gables Elementary School. You have been partners in your children's education and a great support system for our staff. As we come to the end of the school year, we want you to know that your contributions served to enhance the outstanding academic success of our students. We are proud of them and their parents!

Graduation will be held on June 24 at 7:30 p.m. The ceremony will take place in our auditorium. Due to space limitations, each graduate will receive only three tickets. If this presents a problem, please call me, and I'll attempt to secure additional tickets from those families who are not using their quota.

Girls should wear simple dresses and boys dress slacks and shirts with ties. Please avoid gowns, high heels, corsages, and flowers since we want the ceremony to be appropriate for our age group. The children should report at 7 p.m., a half hour before their parents, for us to take attendance and prepare them for the processional.

We wish you all a happy and healthy summer vacation. As educators we recommend that you encourage your child to read while on vacation. Attached to this letter you will find two comprehensive reading lists. One is for children in grades 1–3 and the other for children in grades 4–6. We have worked cooperatively with our local librarians, and they have placed all of these books on a special shelf for the summer vacation period. We request that families take their children to the library and encourage them to sign out these books. The summer is a wonderful time for parents to help improve their child's reading skills.

One of our major goals this year was to have all children feel proud about their heritage. The olympics highlighted the beauty of each nation's culture and the contributions of their famous citizens. Our teachers have selected books that describe the many immigrant families that have become a valuable part of U.S. society. We sincerely hope that by reading these books our children will feel comfortable with who they are and gain a renewed respect and admiration for the families of their classmates. We want our entire community to think of our school as a multicultural family.

We are fortunate to work in this caring community. I will be back at work during the last 3 weeks in August. Please call me if you have any questions or concerns about the new school year.

Sincerely,
Ms. Jane Carter, Principal

The final letter would probably be sent during the week following the last day of school. It is more than a thank-you note to staff. The letter should be the principal's attempt to both compliment and inspire the faculty. If the epigraph at the beginning of this chapter is to come alive, principals have to articulate the pride they feel in being a member of the profession and the admiration they have for their colleagues. We believe the final letter that we present captures this imposing challenge.

North Gables Elementary School
555 Main Street
Gables, Texas 12345
Jane Carter
Principal
Re Year-End

Dear Colleagues,

This has been an exhilarating academic year due to your commitment to our children and dedication to your professional responsibilities. Recently, I came to the realization that I am a leader of leaders. The creative ideas and helpful suggestions provided by the members of our staff have significantly improved our school's program and the tone of the building. Your constructive criticism often convinced me to reassess my positions and often served to improve my professional practices. Your input proved that the whole is greater than the sum of its parts.

We provide our children with much more than an excellent educational institution. In an era marked by violence, tension, and uncertainty, our school became an oasis of sanity. Through your collective efforts our students were able to learn in a secure and supportive environment. Our parents' accolades provided us with a well-deserved vocal support system.

You helped provide our students with the opportunity to participate in several programs that served to expand their academic horizons. These multicultural events influenced many children to volunteer to assist the less fortunate members of our society and to reach out to classmates in need. Others profess to educate the whole child, but our staff made a concerted effort to maximize our students' achievement while giving additional emphasis to the challenge of making them caring human beings. In my opinion, that sets this faculty apart and makes you a model for others to emulate. I look forward to working with you all when we establish the multicultural library that we plan to open next year. That's another indication that this staff always seeks ways to improve our professional practices.

I hope that you and yours have a wonderful, well-deserved vacation. You should be proud of all that was accomplished this year. I am indeed fortunate to be a part of this wonderful staff.

If you are in the area, I'll be working the last 3 weeks of August and would be pleased if you came in to visit. Enjoy the vacation, and I'll write again toward the end of the summer to discuss next year's school-opening procedures.

Sincerely,
Ms. Jane Carter, Principal

RECOMMENDED SUMMER READING FOR GRADES 1–3

Abuela, by Arthur Dorros: Spanish grandmother and granddaughter's story.
African Brothers and Sisters, by Virginia Kroll: Learning about people who live in Africa.

All Kinds of Families, by Norman Simon: Shows many kinds of family life.

Asher and the Cap Maker, by Eric A. Kimmel: A Hanukkah story.

A Birthday Basket for Tia, by Pat Mora: An aunt's love for her little niece.

Borreguita and the Coyote: A Tale from Ayulta, Mexico, by Verna Aadema: A Mexican folk story.

Chinese New Year, by Tricia Brown: Pictures of this Chinese holiday.

Christmas Guest, by David LaRochelle: A visit by a surprise guest at Christmas.

The Day of Ahmed's Secret, by Florence Parry Heide and Judith Heide Gilliland: Egyptian boy's life.

Everybody Cooks Rice, by Norah Dooley: Different cultures and different ways to prepare rice.

Friends in the Park, by Rochelle Bunnett: Special-needs children playing together.

Harriet Tubman: The Road to Freedom, by Rae Bains: The underground railroad for helping slaves escape.

Happy Birthday, Martin Luther King, by Jean Marzollo: Life story of the civil rights leader.

Immigrant Girl, by Brett Harvey: The immigration saga.

James the Vine Puller, by Martha Bennett Stiles: A Brazilian story about getting along with others.

Peppe the Lamplighter, by Elisa Bartone: Every job is important.

Rag Coat, by Lauren Mills: The person is more important than his or her clothes.

St. Patrick's Day, by Gail Gibbons: The story of the Irish holiday.

Siobhan's Journey, by Barbara Beirne: An Irish girl's summer visit to New Jersey.

Stone Soup, by John Warren Stewig: Shows that selfishness is evil.

Tar Beach, by Faith Ringgold: A young Harlem girl's dreams.

Tet: The New Year, by Kim Lan Tran: Vietnamese New Year holiday.

Too Many Tamales, by Gary Soto: A Mexican American family celebration.

Why Am I Different, by Norma Simon: Trying to understand others and yourself.

Why the Sky Is Far Away, by Mary Joan Gerson: A Nigerian folktale.

RECOMMENDED SUMMER READING FOR GRADES 4–6

American Tall Tales, by Mary Pope Osborn: Short stories of American folk heroes.

Celebrating Kwanzaa, by Diane Hoyt Goldsmith: Kwanzaa told in the words of a young child.

Cesar Chavez, by Ruth Franchere: Biography of Mexican American labor leader.

Cherokee Summer, by Diane Hoyt Goldsmith: Struggle between Cherokee and American cultures.

Child of the Owl, by Laurence Yep: Learning to be a Chinese American.

The Devil's Arithmetic, by Jane Yolen: Learning to remember and value your family's roots.

The Friendship, by Mildred D. Taylor: Children learn to face racism.

Going Home, by Nicholosa Mohr: A visit to Puerto Rico during the summer school's vacation.

The House I Live In: At Home in America, by Isadore Seltzer: The United States is made up of many houses.

Jar of Dreams, by Yoshiko Uchida: Coping with racial prejudice and poverty.

Kinaalda, by Monty Roessel: A coming of age ceremony for a young Navajo.

A Migrant Family, by Larry Dane Brimner: Life of migrant laborers.

People, by Peter Spier: Story about the similarities and differences among all the people in the world.

The People Who Hugged the Trees, by Deborah Lee Rose: An ancient folk story from India.

Song of the Chirimia, by Jane Anne Volkner: A folktale from Guatemala.

Spanish-American Folktales, by Teresa Pijoan: Many tales about Spanish American culture.

Spring Festivals, by Mike Rosen: The ways many cultures celebrate spring.

Tongues of Jade, by Laurence Yep: Many Chinese American folktales.

Totem Pole, by Diane Hoyt Goldsmith: How an Indian carves a totem pole for his tribe.

Who Belongs Here? An American Story, by Margy Burns Knight: Intolerance in America.

CHAPTER 15

A Model School District Program

Many of the techniques we've discussed have been used in the Freeport School District. The community reflects immigration patterns similar to those confronting educators throughout the United States. We believe those in the district have very effectively responded to their foreign-born students and their parents. Their programs serve as a model for us all, and we particularly applaud their continuing efforts to develop a more sophisticated level of practice. We asked them to document their extraordinary efforts to help new arrivals to their school and community, and we present their response here.

Freeport, New York, is a community with a rich nautical history. The village, incorporated in 1892, was settled by the Meroke Indians. The tribe found the bay and streams rich in fish for food and shells for wampum. In 1659 Edward Raynor arrived and cleared land for homes and called the area Great South Woods. In 1853 it was renamed Freeport, a nickname used by fisherman during colonial times who landed their cargo without paying customs duties. Oystering was a thriving industry after the Civil War but declined in the early part of the 20th century due to pollution. A rail line and Woodcleft Canal, dredged in 1868, and other canals led to a population boom. According to historical accounts, the early boaters attracted to Freeport were smugglers and rumrunners. Today, the charter fishing boats and seafood restaurants are the reason visitors flock to Freeport.

There was no shortage of ways for visitors or residents to get to the waterfront or the beach. The trolley traversed the community to the water and the short-lived Freeport Railroad ran trains from Sunrise Highway to the waterfront in 1913. Cartoonist Fontaine Fox supposedly used it as the inspiration for his famous "Toonerville Trolley." In addition, ferries transported people to and from Point Lookout Beach. Just after World War I, shipyards built a small industry in Freeport. This ended in the 1960s, at which time boat dealerships appeared and continue a brisk business today.

The 1940s saw the Nautical Mile become a place for dining and celebrity sightings. Guy Lombardo opened East Point Restaurant. Lombardo was not the first show-business star to live in Freeport. In 1910 vaudeville actors established an artist colony. They founded the Long Island Good Hearted Thespian Society, which built a club and presented shows during the summer for more than a decade. Actors Broderick Crawford and Susan Sullivan called Freeport home, along with Branch Rickey, owner of the Brooklyn Dodgers. The late television programmer Brandon Tartikoff, the late TV sports commentator Dick Schaap, and gossip columnist Cindy Adams grew up in Freeport and graduated from Freeport High School.

As early as 1905 Blacks lived in Freeport but were restricted to living in the area near the railroad tracks. The Ku Klux Klan kept them out of other areas. It wasn't until 1967 that Black families moved into otherwise White neighborhoods. Freeport was one of the first school systems in New York to voluntarily desegregate its schools. One of the ways this was done was through the creation of a pre-K–kindergarten center at the almost all-Black Columbus Avenue School. The Atkinson School became the only school for grades 5 and 6. Freeport is the first district to develop a magnet-school system for grades 1 through 4. Each school has a theme and parents choose which school their child will attend.

The ethnic shift began again in the 1980s with large numbers of Hispanic families moving to Freeport. In the 1990s there was a marked increase. By 2003 more than one-third of the 7,056 students in the Freeport public schools were of Hispanic descent, with one-third of these children in English language learner (ELL) classes. More than half of the 2,000 adults who attend English-speakers-of-other-languages (ESOL), general equivalency diploma (GED), or citizenship classes identified themselves as either Hispanic or Latino. The district is racially balanced, comprising one-third White (not including Hispanic), one-third Black, and one-third Hispanic.

Recognizing that the immigrant population had a special set of needs, the district began providing not only education but support and communication to make the transition easier for new residents. This is seen across the board, from pre-K through adult education. One of the first things that began to happen was the translation of all notices, flyers, application forms, newsletters, letters, brochures, and forms to both English and Spanish.

Bilingual and ESL teachers conduct parental information meetings and communicate regularly in the native language, orally and in writing, to parents about their children's progress. The Central Registry Office has two bilingual clerks. This enables those registering children to answer questions and effectively direct parents to appropriate departments or personnel for assistance. There is also a bilingual community worker who makes home visits as needed.

Each of the eight school buildings and the superintendent's office has a kit called the Talk System that makes direct translations possible when a translator is present. This technology is used to transmit the communication electronically to audience members holding receivers at meetings held at the school and district levels by principals, PTAs, and the board and any informational event sponsored by the district.

Translations are done by a variety of school personnel, one full-time translator, a bilingual school-community liaison, bilingual teachers, social workers, school psychologists, teacher assistants, secretaries, and other school personnel. Translations can then be done for school registration for teachers and administrators with parents who require assistance.

Freeport High School conducts an annual Spanish Parents Guidance Night where four bilingual guidance counselors give information on understanding the report card, the attendance policy, courses (the Freeport High School course catalogue is in Spanish), and promotion and graduation requirements, as well as information about college, including financial aid, the admission process, college selection, and career guidance.

There is an active Latino Club in the high school whose events include cultural activities throughout the year, such as celebrating Hispanic holidays, sharing regional cuisine, and learning about the unique customs of Latin American countries. Scholarship opportunities for Hispanic students are part of many scholarship announcements.

The magnet schools for grades 1 through 4 have developed their own style for helping both parents and students. At the New Visions School, parenting workshops conducted in Spanish are taking place. Workshops include health and nutrition, homework tips, and basic parenting skills. In addition, the school nurse and social worker assist parents in obtaining health insurance through state and federal programs.

Both the social worker and the school psychologist at New Visions are bilingual and are an important link between the school, community, and the Spanish-speaking home. Many of the parents themselves have never been to school or have had little experience with school and therefore need help navigating the system. In addition, the climate is new to many of these immigrant parents. The support staff alerts them that their children will need coats in the winter. Although this seems like a simple concept, it is one of the many social, emotional, physical, and financial aspects of day-to-day support that the school is offering families.

One reality of life for the parents is their inability to function well in an English-speaking environment. It is necessary to empower them with the tools they need; therefore adult continuing-education classes are held in the evening to teach parents English. Coupled with these classes is a day care worker who helps their children with their homework and often accompanies them to class. This is a win-win for the parent and child. Both get the assistance they need.

It is our hope that, by opening classes in the magnet schools for parents of the students, the students will see that the parents value education, and the parents will feel comfortable in the school setting, will be encouraged to take part in their children's education and take pride in their schoolwork, and will learn valuable parenting skills. Finally, these parents attend PTA meetings in the building during part of their class time. We hope they will understand they are both valued and welcome as participants in the education of the children.

There are also classes every day for parents of our preschool and kindergarten population. Parents attend ESOL and GED classes every day and their children ages 3 and 4 attend also. While the parents are learning, so are the children. It is an opportunity for them to learn English and gain basic words and terms for colors, food, and clothing. We find that many of these children also need help with separation and how to use new toys and games.

The Archer Street School, a magnet school for grades 1 through 4, has a We Share Books program. This program encourages families to read together. The teachers make every effort to send books home in the child's native language.

Parenting workshops address the needs of the multicultural community by presenting these sessions in both English and Spanish. The Parenting Center houses materials for parents in both languages.

Archer Street School is the home of the Freeport School District's newcomers class. This class is for youngsters in grades 1 and 2 who enter the district directly from their native country.

The Puente Program is a series of parent-child gatherings held in the evenings at Archer that address the needs of the Hispanic population. Spanish is the only language spoken at these workshops. Bilingual and ESL teacher assistants volunteer their time to demonstrate and teach parents strategies to improve their child's language arts skills. Oral language arts and appreciation of literature are the focus.

Atkinson School has implemented a new program that has improved the outreach to impoverished families. The school-based program Family Intervention Through School (FITS) is a grant-funded initiative involving a collaborative effort between the Freeport schools and South Nassau Communities Hospital.

The program targets children from low-income families who are experiencing difficulties in school adjustment and participation or exhibit signs of emotional distress. FITS is offered to those families who meet the TANF (Temporary Assistance to Needy Families) requirements.

Once children are identified as candidates by staff personnel, they are referred to FITS through a school psychologist or social worker. Upon receipt of a referral, the specialists determine which families are eligible for these services. Specialists arrange for the families to receive necessary services. It was anticipated that by helping these families obtain various services and psychological assistance, there would be a marked improvement in the child's current performance and an avoidance of future difficulties. A key component of the program is the outreach to our Hispanic families, especially with the inclusion of Spanish staff who are available to work during and after the school day. Many of the parents who would not be normally be helped were assisted via this program.

There is also a wide range of services and parenting skills workshops held. These workshops are conducted in English and Spanish separately to reach all parents.

To make new students to this country feel comfortable, Atkinson School has implemented a weekly guidance session with a bilingual teacher. It is designed especially for those students who have left family behind to live in a new country as a result of a divorce or economic necessity.

The district's administration has also reached out to the Hispanic community. Regular meetings are held with various community-based Hispanic leaders, central-administration personnel, and building principals to get their perceptions and to discover their needs. A list of concerns and possible solutions have been gleaned from these meetings. It is also a way to disseminate information among the different groups, so that they understand how committed the district is to the children and their parents.

The converse is also true. It is an opportunity to educate the leaders about school regulations and policies. It enables the school leaders to discuss how the administrators can help us, help families by giving them information that they seem not to understand. This continued dialogue makes success for these families a more realistic goal.

The district has a number of administrators on the Nassau County Task Force on Gangs. Because some gang members are Hispanic, it gives the administration insight into these potential problems. We are part of the community-wide initiative to solve the problem and attempt to educate children and their parents about evils of gang membership.

The Freeport Dual Language Program was started in 1993 and involves children in pre-K through grade 6 who speak English or Spanish as native languages. The goal is to place both groups of children together in a learning environment where two languages are used to teach the regular curriculum. Native English-speaking children learn a second language early while their native Spanish-speaking counterparts acquire English. Dual-language students are taught by two teachers, in two different classrooms, one bilingual and one monolingual, who work together in a team-teaching arrangement. Another key goal of the program is to increase cultural awareness for all of the participants. Parents and children of two languages and cultures interact and learn from each other throughout the school year, each group making a unique contribution to the other.

Administrators and staff members continue to explore many avenues to achieve the vision to inspire in all the desire to learn and succeed. Our schools will be safe learning communities that celebrate our achievements and encourage active partnerships with families and the entire community. We will empower students to embrace the challenges and the opportunities of the future. We will achieve the goal to leave behind no child or parent.

CHAPTER 16

Epilogue

Educating the mind, without educating the heart, is no education at all.

—Aristotle

We believe, as stated in our introduction, that our strategies for reaching out to the Hispanic population would be of value when we work with all immigrant populations. The educational process should begin with our responsibility to learn about the culture and mores of all of our students. Staff members often take great pleasure in getting to know recently arrived immigrant families and report that children and parents usually relate interesting experiences about their homeland. Their struggles to reach our shores are poignant and inspirational and serve to get our less enthusiastic staff members involved and more motivated in our mission. Those of us committed to the task learned that changing the attitudes of some faculty and residents was as difficult as gaining the confidence of the new arrivals to our community.

We also have an obligation to help them feel themselves to be a part of the community. This will occur only when the indigenous citizens truly believe there is value in involving the new arrivals in all aspects of community life. Being a resident who merely observes another culture is not the same as being part of its daily life and traditions. The observer resides in a ghetto. The participant is mainstreamed and included.

The vignettes in this epilogue were part of our in-service program for our staff. The beauty of the Native American culture helped teachers to address their own stereotypes and to appreciate many aspects of an Indian child's basic upbringing and initial education. Likewise, learning about the traditions and sophistication of aspects of the African heritage allowed educators to see beyond the stifling era of slavery, which continues to contribute to the stereotype of Black Americans.

The epilogue is not an afterthought. It is our way of stressing the responsibility of educational leaders to view new minority populations as an exciting challenge. It is our hope that when reviewing our programs, activities, and strategies, each educator will consider our recommendations and then use those that will be most effective with their own constituency. We hope that the methods described to involve the newly arrived children and families will be received as a gift from all of the caring colleagues who collaborated in our project.

Contemporary schools are populated by an ever-changing student body. Traditionally, in most areas our teachers were predominantly White women and our students were American born and the children of second- and third-generation European immigrants. Foreign-speaking minority children were a rarity, and the schools had few programs to address their needs. In the Southwest, Mexicans came across the border, creating the challenge of a Spanish-speaking minority. Asian children lived in enclaves in New York and California, but little was done to involve their families in their school's daily operation. There were other areas whose schools were populated by newly arrived European, Asian, and African American children, but educators did little to adjust their teaching techniques or to differentiate instruction. These youngsters were expected to endure the same curriculum and teaching methods being offered to more affluent and better-educated children. Their unique needs were largely disregarded, and they were taught traditional lessons and judged by the standards of their more articulate classmates.

Today the 50 largest American cities presently have minority populations that are a statistical majority. For the first time in our country's history, the White male no longer comprises 50% of the workforce. Women and minorities will shortly make up almost 65% of our laborers. Business reformers have addressed many of the concerns of women in the area of employment, most particularly their traditional lack of promotional opportunity. Over the last few decades educators have examined how males and females were treated in schools and, in conjunction with activist groups such as the National Organization of Women, brought about major attitudinal changes. In the field of business, the glass ceiling has been breached and many women are being appointed to leadership positions. These are worthy achievements, but we have not witnessed an equal intensity in proactive programs and strategies for our foreign-language-speaking children. If as predicted they become a vital part of our nation's workforce, we had better make it a priority to provide them with the necessary educational skills to succeed.

Immigrant parents remain reluctant to attend open-school nights or PTA meetings and even more hesitant to make contact with teachers to ascertain their child's progress. Educators often tacitly accept this shortcoming and frequently do little to try to understand the culture of the community they are serving. Principals should be dedicated to solving problems and should not accept this lack of partnership with their foreign-born residents. Not recognizing the limitations of this poor parental involvement is indicative of a principal who is coasting. In this regard, principals must use their bridge-building skills and should enthusiastically explore ways to reach out to this segment of their school populations. They would do well to remember the powerful educational leadership maxim "When principals coast, they can only go downhill!"

Drawing on our own personal experiences as administrators, we share our school district's attempt to involve our foreign-born parents. Our student body included a sizable Portuguese population who, like the parents of their Hispanic counterparts in other districts, were not actively involved in the school community. The faculty had frequently discussed this and found it convenient to put the blame on the foreign-born parents. Negative statements about the community's lack of participation in school affairs went unchallenged and eventually were accepted as being true. We conveniently forgot our responsibility as educators and change agents. Over lunch one day the issue was resurrected when a teacher complained about not being able to contact a parent. It was agreed to make our tacit acceptance of the dilemma the subject of the next faculty meeting.

Our staff opened the meeting by citing the following concerns:

1. Foreign-born parents were not attending conferences or team meetings.
2. These parents were difficult to contact since they were employed

during the day, and when teachers called in the evenings, no one
at home spoke English.

3. Very few of them had joined the PTA.
4. They rarely attended student scheduling conferences with the
   guidance counselors.
5. They did not respond to written letters, progress reports, report
   cards, or invitations to meetings.

The staff had an animated discussion since it was the first time we
had openly acknowledged that the Portuguese community's lack of
participation was also our problem, and we recognized we had done
little to improve the situation. Some continued to blame the parents,
but others began to make suggestions. There was clearly a lack of una-
nimity, but the meeting was emotional and maintained everyone's
interest. As the time came to end the session, many remained frustrated
because there wasn't one strategy that achieved consensus. The
teacher-union president, who happened to be a member of the staff,
asked when the next PTA meeting would be held. When she heard the
date, she said, "I will bring a Portuguese parent to the next meeting,
and I hope each of you will do the same thing." Thirty-seven teachers
escorted our foreign-born parents to the next PTA meeting.

As a result of that meeting, the following was achieved:

1. We received the names of several parents who would serve as
   translators during parent-teacher conferences. One volunteer
   turned out to be a college professor who was articulate in both
   languages.
2. All correspondence to parents who spoke only Portuguese at
   home would be written in both languages.
3. All 37 parents joined the PTA, and one was appointed to assist
   the corresponding secretary.
4. Outreach methods to foreign-born community clubs and businesses were established and the teachers involved would inform
   the organizations about forthcoming school activities.
5. One of the parents volunteered to start a Portuguese dance club
   so students could perform and celebrate their cultural skills.

The ripple effects of that faculty meeting had districtwide ramifications. Less than a decade later one of our Portuguese parents became a board of education member, and shortly thereafter she became its president. It led us to believe that school administrators must be proactive when addressing the needs of their non-English-speaking residents.

Staff members expressed guilt about the length of time it took for us to confront the fact that a large segment of our population was not comfortable with becoming active with our school. As the school's leaders, we had to accept responsibility for not recognizing that it was a problem awaiting a viable plan and creative solution. One had to believe that we had simply just touched the surface of our foreign-born parents' reluctance in dealing with the school and its personnel. A committee was established to explore the needs of these parents and also to provide in-service and sensitivity training for the entire staff.

We realized that all immigrants bring their own traditions with them when they arrive in America and our school personnel had not given them any opportunity to showcase their culture. What's more, the system rarely educated our teachers about these vital characteristics. Thus our staff and foreign-born youngsters were unable to inform their classmates about the pride they felt in the achievements of their ancestors. Our committee did not want to be guilty of preaching to our colleagues. We feared our colleagues would perceive us as haughty, and we were even more concerned that we would seem to be minimizing and rejecting their former efforts. Thus we created a newsletter that our committee selected pertinent articles for to provoke discussion and continue our momentum.

In an issue of *Teacher* magazine, we discovered an article by Robert Lake (1990), a Native American, that we believed would help us take a giant step forward in our in-service program. Truthfully, those of us on the committee benefited from reading the article as much as those we hoped to influence. Robert Lake, whose Indian name is Medicine Grizzly Bear, talks about his son, Wind-Wolf, who has begun attending public school for the first time. His letter to the teacher is reproduced here in its entirety.

Dear Teacher,

I would like to introduce you to my son, Wind-Wolf. He is probably what you consider a typical Indian kid. He was born and raised on the reservation. He has black hair, dark brown eyes, and an olive complexion. And like so many Indian children his age, he is shy and quiet in the classroom. He is 5 years old, in kindergarten, and I can't understand why you have already labeled him a "slow learner."

At the age of 5, he has already been through quite an education compared with his peers in Western society. As his first introduction into the world, he was bonded to his mother and the Mother Earth in a traditional native childbirth ceremony. And he has been continuously cared for by his mother, father, brothers, sisters, cousins, aunts, uncles, grandparents, and extended tribal family since this ceremony.

From his mother's warm and loving arms, Wind-Wolf was placed in a secure and specially designed Indian baby basket. His father and the medicine elders conducted another ceremony with him that served to bond him with the essence of his genetic Father, the Great Spirit, the Grandfather Sun and the Grandmother Moon. This was all done to introduce him properly into the new and natural world, not the world of artificiality, and to protect his sensitive and delicate soul. It is our people's way of showing the newborn respect, ensuring that he starts his life on the path of spirituality.

The traditional Indian baby basket became his "turtle's shell" and served as the first seat of his classroom. He was strapped in for safety, protected from injury by the willow roots and hazel wood construction. The basket was made by a tribal elder who had gathered her materials with prayer and in a ceremonial way. It is the same kind of basket our people have used for thousands of years. It is specially designed to provide a child with the kind of knowledge and experience he will need in order to survive in his culture and environment.

Wind-Wolf was strapped in snugly with a deliberate restriction upon his arms and legs. Although you in Western society may argue that such a method serves to hinder motor-skill development and abstract reasoning, we believe it forces the child to first develop his intuitive faculties, rational intellect, symbolic thinking, and five senses. Wind-Wolf was with his mother constantly, closely bonding physically, as she carried him on her back or held him in front while breast-feeding. She carried him everywhere she went, and every night he slept with both his parents. Because of this, Wind-Wolf's emotional setting wasn't only a secure environment, but it was also very colorful, complicated, sensitive, and diverse. He has been with his mother at the ocean at daybreak when she made her prayers and gathered fresh seaweed from the rocks, he has sat with his uncles in a rowboat on the river while they fished with gill nets, and he has watched and listened to elders as they told creation stories and animal legends and sang songs around the campfires.

He has attended the sacred and ancient White Deerskin Dance of his people and is well acquainted with the cultures and languages of other tribes. He has been with his mother when she gathered herbs for healing and watched his tribal aunts and grandmothers gather and prepare traditional foods such as acorn, smoked salmon, eel, and deer meat. He has played with abalone shells, pine nuts, iris grass string, and leather while watching the women make beaded jewelry and traditional native regalia. He has had many opportunities to watch his father, uncles, and ceremonial leaders use different kinds of colorful feathers and sing different songs while preparing for the sacred dances and rituals.

As he grew older, Wind-Wolf began to crawl out of the baby basket, develop his motor skills, and explore the world around him. When frightened or sleepy, he could always return to the basket, as a turtle withdraws into its shell. Such an inward journey allows one to reflect in privacy on what he has learned and to carry the new knowledge deeply into the unconscious and the soul. Shapes, sizes, colors, textures, sound, smell, feeling, and taste foster the learning process and therefore functionally integrate the physical and spiritual, matter and energy, conscious and unconscious, individual and social.

This kind of learning goes beyond the basics of distinguishing the differences between rough and smooth, square and round, hard and soft, black and white, similarities and extremes.

For example, Wind-Wolf was with his mother in South Dakota while she danced for seven days straight in the hot sun, fasting and piercing herself in the sacred Sun Dance Ceremony of a distant tribe. He has been doctored in a number of different healing ceremonies by medicine men and women from diverse places ranging from Alaska and Arizona to New York and California. He has been in more than 20 different sweat lodge rituals used by native tribes to purify mind, body, and soul since he was 3 years old. He has already been exposed to many different racial brothers: Protestant, Catholic, Asian, Buddhist, and Tibetan Lamaist.

It takes a long time to absorb and reflect on these kinds of experiences, so maybe that is why you think my Indian child is a slow learner. His aunts and grandmothers taught him to count and know his numbers while they sorted out the complex materials used to make the abstract designs in native baskets. He listened to his mother count every bead and sort out numerically according to color while she painstakingly made complex beaded belts and necklaces.

He learned his basic numbers by helping his father count and sort rocks to be used in the sweat lodge—7 rocks for a medicine sweat, say, or 13 for the summer solstice ceremony. (The rocks are later heated and doused with water to create purifying steam.) And he was taught to learn mathematics by counting the sticks we use in our native hand game. So I realize he may be slow in grasping the methods and tools that you are using in your classroom, ones quite familiar to his white peers, but I hope you will be patient with him. It takes time to adjust to a new cultural system and learn new things.

He is not "culturally disadvantaged," but he is "culturally different." If you ask him how many months there are in a year, he will probably tell you 13. He will respond this way not because he doesn't know how to count properly, but because he has been taught by our traditional people that there are 13 full moons in a year according to the native tribal calendar and that there are really 13 planets in our solar system and 13 tail feathers on a perfectly balanced eagle, the most powerful kind of bird to use in ceremony and healing.

But he also knows that some eagles may only have 12 tail feathers, or 7, that they do not all have the same number. He knows that the flicker has exactly 10 tail feathers; that [they] are red and black, representing the directions of east and west, life and death; and that this bird is considered a "fire" bird, a power used in native doctoring and healing. He can probably count more than 40 different kinds of birds, tell you and his peers what kind of bird each is and where it lives, the seasons in which it appears, and how it is used in a sacred ceremony.

He may have trouble writing his name on a piece of paper, but he knows how to say it and many other things in several different Indian languages. He is not fluent yet because he is only 5 years old and required by law to attend your educational system, learn your language, your values, your ways of thinking, and your methods of teaching and learning.

So you see, all of these influences together make him somewhat shy and quiet and perhaps "slow" according to your standards. But if Wind-Wolf was not prepared for his first tentative foray into your world, neither were you appreciative of his culture. On the first day of class, you had difficulty with his name. You wanted to call him Wind, insisting that Wolf somehow must be his middle name. The students in the class laughed at him, causing further embarrassment.

While you are trying to teach him your new methods, helping him to learn new tools for self-discovery and adapt to his new learning environment, he may be looking out the window as if daydreaming. Why? Because he has been taught to watch and study the changes in nature.

It is hard for him to make the appropriate psychic switch from the right to the left hemisphere of the brain when he sees the leaves turning colors, the geese heading south, and the squirrels scurrying around to get ready for a harsh winter. In his heart, in his young mind, and almost by instinct, he knows that this is the time of year he is supposed to be with his people gathering and preparing fish, deer meat, and native plants and herbs, and learning his assigned tasks in this role.

He is caught between two worlds, torn by two distinct cultural systems. Yesterday, for the third time in 2 weeks, he came home crying and said he wanted to have his hair cut. He says he doesn't have any friends at school because they make fun of his long hair. I tried to explain to him that in our culture, long hair is a sign of masculinity and balance and is a source of power. But he remained adamant in his position.

To make matters worse, he recently encountered his first harsh case of racism. Wind-Wolf had managed to adopt at least one good friend at school. On the way home from school one day, he asked his new pal if he wanted to come home and play with him until supper.

That was okay with Wind-Wolf's mother, who was walking with them. When they got to the little friend's house, the two boys ran inside to ask permission while Wind-Wolf's mother waited.

But the other boy's mother lashed out: "It is OK if you play with him at school, but we don't allow those kind of people in our house!" When my wife asked why not, the other boy's mother answered, "Because you are Indians and we are white, and I don't want my kids growing up with your kind of people."

So now my young Indian child does not want to go to school anymore (even though we cut his hair). He feels that he does not belong. He is the only Indian child in your class, and is well aware of the fact. Instead of being proud of his race, heritage, and culture, he feels ashamed. When he watches television, he asks why the white people hate us so much and always kill our people in the movies and why they take everything away from us. He asks why the other kids in school are not taught about the power, beauty, and essence of nature or provided with an opportunity to experience the world around them firsthand. He says he hates living in the city and that he misses his Indian cousins and friends. He asks why one young white girl at school who is his friend tells him, "I like you, Wind-Wolf, because you are a good Indian."

Now he refuses to sing his native songs, play with his Indian artifacts, learn his language, or participate in his sacred ceremonies. When I ask him to go to an urban powwow or help me with a sacred sweat-house lodge ritual, he says no because "that's weird," and he doesn't want his friends at school to think he doesn't believe in God.

So dear teacher, I want to introduce you to my son Wind-Wolf, who is not really a "typical" little Indian kid after all. He stems from a long line of hereditary chiefs, medicine men and women, and ceremonial leaders whose accomplishments and unique forms of knowledge are still being studied and recorded in contemporary books. He has seven different tribal systems flowing through his blood; he is even part white. I want my child to succeed in school and life. I don't want him to be a dropout or juvenile delinquent or to end up on drugs and alcohol because he is made to feel inferior or because of discrimination. I want him to be proud of his rich heritage and culture, and I would like him to develop necessary capabilities to adapt to and succeed in both cultures. But I need your help.

What you say and what you do in the classroom, what you teach and how you teach it, and what you don't say and don't teach will have a significant effect on the potential success or failure of my child. Please remember that this is the primary year of his education. All I ask is that you work with me, not against me, to help my child in the best way. If you don't have the knowledge, preparation, experience, or training to effectively deal with culturally different children, I am willing to help you with the few resources I have available or will direct you to such resources.

Millions of dollars have been appropriated by Congress and are being spent each year for "Indian Education." All you have to do is take advantage of it and encourage your school to make an effort to use it in the name of "equal education." My Indian child has a constitutional right to learn, retain, and maintain his heritage and culture. By the same token, I strongly believe that non-Indian children also have a constitutional right to learn about Native American heritage and culture, because Indians play a significant part in the history of Western society. Until this reality is equally understood and applied in education as a whole, there will be a lot more children in grades K–2 identified as "slow learners."

My son, Wind-Wolf, is not an empty glass coming into your class to be filled. He is a full basket coming into a different environment and society with something special to share. Please let him share his knowledge, heritage, and culture with you and his peers.

The impact of Wind-Wolf's experiences continues to reverberate in our hearts and minds. In discussing them with educators, we discovered they were equally moved emotionally and wanted to confront their unintentional blindness to the needs of children and parents of the foreign born. In dissecting the stories, we recognized there was much work to be done. Listing some of the cogent observations and suggestions from these two vignettes and the one that follows provided us with a guide toward our in-service needs and the vision for this book. It became obvious that the techniques we were developing would serve all immigrant populations since the premise was to research and celebrate their culture, heroes, and past achievements.

Our observations were often accompanied by personal experience provided by a staff member or from our research. When we stressed the necessity of understanding the culture of our immigrant population, a police officer told the story of one of his colleagues who had stopped a young Chinese man for a traffic violation. As the officer interrogated the driver, the young man looked at his feet and avoided direct eye contact. The officer was not going to give him a citation and planned to let him go with a warning. However, the young man's behavior annoyed the policeman. Suddenly he took the young lad by the shoulders and shouted, "Won't you have the decency to look at me when I'm talking to you!" What he didn't understand was the Chinese culture. The driver was showing the utmost respect since, in his community, eye-to-eye contact is considered impolite and disrespectful. This incident led to an in-service course at the local police academy titled Respecting Different Cultures and Antibias Training.

What's more, one of us met with a professor at a local university who shared additional information about the culture of our Chinese students. These ideas were part of a multicultural course taught by several professors at C. W. Post, Long Island University.

1. Traditional Chinese culture and customs
   A. Chinese society and family emphasize respect for elders and authority.
   B. Family value is above individual importance. Family duties are above individual desire.
   C. Chinese culture demands obedience; a good child is an obedient child.
   D. Traditional Chinese parents tend to value boys more than girls. The oldest son is afforded special importance in a hierarchy of siblings.
   E. Chinese people generally have difficulty accepting the existence of psychological problems. They tend to think of psychological problems as physical problems.
   F. Chinese parents do not involve themselves in school-related matters.

2. Characteristics of traditional Chinese students
   A. Chinese students are generally not comfortable with direct eye contact when speaking to an authority figure. This does not mean the student is not listening or does not respect the person speaking. In Chinese culture, it is not polite for a person of lower status to look a person of higher status directly in the eye.
   B. Chinese students tend to be inhibited in expressing feelings. They seldom show their emotions.
   C. Chinese students are generally less independent in decision making as compared with American students.
   D. Chinese students seem to have a low tolerance for ambiguity.
   E. Chinese students tend to be passive.
3. Learning style of traditional Chinese students
   A. Chinese students tend to be shy and self-conscious when expressing ideas in front of groups.
   B. Chinese students like classes that are formal in structure rather than informal free-expression formats.
   C. Chinese students find it difficult to respond to spontaneous questioning.
   D. Chinese students prefer to major in engineering and science and tend to shy away from social studies and literature.
   E. Chinese students do not feel comfortable in disagreeing with the teacher and other students in class discussions and debates.

Our staff members taught very few Chinese and Asian students. However, they believed that this information should have been part of their teacher training at the university level or in district in-service courses. Many were disappointed in how they approached the few Chinese students in their classes. Obviously, their attempts to communicate with these children's parents were equally unproductive.

It became patently clear that even our social studies staff knew little about the cultural contributions of different minority groups. If they didn't major in the history of a particular continent or nation, they had little formal training in the remaining countries and cultures. We learned that none of our history teachers ever took a class in African history. In their lessons on immigration, they did an excellent job on the immigration of Europeans, less on Asians, and absolutely nothing on Africans. They may have briefly explored the slave trade, but Africans were portrayed as a simple uneducated agricultural people without any worthwhile culture or value to their civilization.

In beginning the study of yet another minority community, we enlisted the support of college teachers of African studies, the National Association for the Advancement of Colored People, and the Anti-Defamation League of B'nai B'rith. We admittedly knew nothing about the Africa that existed before the slave-trade era. This period was completely omitted from school texts on social studies. The Anti-Defamation League sponsors a program called A World of Difference, which is a bias-prevention program with the goal of appreciating the differences of all people. We were referred to the Teacher Corps of the Association of Teacher Educators in Washington, DC, and were given permission to reproduce the very poignant article that follows. It was published in Washington, DC, in 1977 and later in 1992.

Many may criticize the inclusion of the plight of African Americans when our main thesis is how to reach out to non-English-speaking children and families. We feel, however, that almost all of our proactive techniques and activities equally apply to immigrants, minority groups, or Native Americans. English-speaking minorities, such as the British and Irish, also needed techniques to help them understand American educational traditions and the means to share the wealth of their culture with the indigenous citizens of their new community.

"AFRICAN ORIGINS"

The first Black immigrants to America were far from being "simple," "naive," "childlike," or "uncivilized" people as they were often portrayed in texts. Nor were they "young" in the ways of civilization. They had experienced a rich history of social, cultural, economic, and political development that began long before many of the civilizations of Western Europe.

By 1441, when the Portuguese left West Africa with the first shipload of slaves, Africa already had seen the rise and fall of many great kingdoms. The earliest centers of African civilization included Kush (modern Northern Sudan) and Axum (modern Ethiopia) in East Africa, the Bantu and Kongo Kingdoms in South and Southeast Africa, and Ghana, Mali, and Songhay in West Africa.

The latter kingdoms were located in that area of the continent which subsequently became the "slaving region" of European traders. These empires had reached their peaks and had begun to decline by the time the American colonies were beginning to be settled. Songhay, the last of the great African kingdoms, ended in 1591, 16 years before the founding of the first English-American colony at Jamestown, Virginia.

The African kingdoms of antiquity were responsible for some remarkable accomplishments in commerce, construction, agriculture, arts and crafts, and education. Blacks helped design and build some of the great Egyptian pyramids. They were among the world's first artists, iron makers, weavers, and users of plants for medicinal and dietary purposes. Antar, the African poet, received acclaim as one of the greatest poets of antiquity. Africans developed well-built cities with great walls, palaces, and temples at Meroe, Kilwa, Zimbabwe, Mbanzo Kongo, Kumbi, Gao, and Timbuktu. These cities became centers of domestic and international activities and of exchange of culture, education, politics, business, and trade.

The first African immigrants to America were far from homogeneous. They came from different countries, tribal groups, and cultural backgrounds; spoke different languages and dialects; and reflected different aspects of the African worldview. Some were royalty, warriors, and statesmen, but most were average citizens, farmers, artisans, and craftsmen. Some were Muslims, but most were ancestor and nature worshippers.

Some came from Northern, Eastern, and Central Africa, but most came from the West Coast. They had known complex social systems and political structures; they had experienced the social demands of accommodating different cultures and peoples encountered through war, trade and travel; and they had known military conquest and enslavement. Initially, African immigrants came to the [N]ew [W]orld not as slaves, but as crew members of Spanish and Portuguese expeditions and as indentured servants. They arrived in Latin America more than 100 years before any slaves came to North America. Even the first 20 Africans who were imported to North America in 1619 were not referred to as "slaves." It was not until the 1640s that slavery began as a legal institution in the English colonies.

Despite the diversity among the original African immigrants, some things in common and shared experiences existed among them. The focal point of their aboriginal lifestyles was the local community organization, centered on a farming economy and an extended family structure. Within this structural framework, cooperation and mutual aid was prized; the wisdom, experience, and authority of elders were revered; cultural values and traditions were transmitted through music, folklore, and dance; priests and griots (oral historians) were the guardians and transmitters of tribal history and traditions; religion, arts, and crafts permeated and reflected everyday life activities; and an approach to life and living existed in which all people and things were intertwined to make for unity and continuity.

These common cultural denominations allowed for a consensus of experiences among the first generations of African immigrants to the New World. They served as unifying forces that helped them endure their particular American experiences. They enabled Black immigrants in various parts of the New World to cooperate in creating new customs, traditions, and values, which reflected their African origins and, yet, made them neither totally African nor fully American, but a combination of both. Thus was created the background for the birth of the Afro-American. (Association of Teacher Educators, 1992)

One of our young social studies teachers overtly rejected our including the plight of African Americans in our research. His feeling, which he expressed quite forcefully, was that since Black citizens were free since the 1860s, they were hardly new immigrants. With all of the economic and political programs that offered them assistance, they should have accomplished more than they have and should certainly be mainstream citizens after more than 140 years of freedom. Some other staff members reminded him about restrictive voting laws, housing exclusions, and racist attitudes that made their integration into mainstream U.S. society difficult, if not impossible. He remained unmoved in his position until an older staff member related the following story.

During World War II, "Negro" soldiers fought in completely segregated outfits and were led by White officers. More shameful was the fact that if African American soldiers were stationed in the Deep South or Southwest, they were not allowed to go into the stores on the base. These facilities were called the post exchange, or PX, by soldiers. However, German prisoners of war were allowed to use these same facilities. Our Black soldiers had to go into town and use the stores run by members of their own race.

Other faculty members reminded our young social studies teacher about segregation on trains and buses. Finally one teacher produced a picture showing water fountains restricted to use by Whites or Blacks and said, "Do you really feel Black Americans were totally freed by the Emancipation Proclamation during the Civil War?" The teacher remained somewhat dubious but did say that perhaps he had not thought the issue through. His mind was opened to another point of view.

As administrators, we remained confident that we all had to begin confronting dormant issues of prejudice that we had filed away in our subconscious. Biased behavior often comes from deep-seated experiences, and this study was going to bring periods of discomfort to many of us. The challenge was to confront these covert feelings and to examine them in light of today's reality and modern research data.

In our exploration of various cultures, we also realized that the era of America as a melting pot was over. We were all taught that, as immigrants, all of our cultural and traditional differences would be "boiled away" when we came to the United States. Somehow we would all emerge as Americans and in a relatively short time we would have a united common heritage. Today we are teaching that our former cultural differences are to be valued as keepsakes and should enhance our pride in our roots. As our population has become richly diversified, our contemporary citizens are portrayed as being a "tossed salad." We are encouraged to take pride in our ancestors and their traditions but enjoy the status of being Americans with equal standing.

We learned that in any analysis of America's changing demographics, educators had to adjust their focus and commit to intense in-service training. Many educators merely mouth that "the only constant in education is change." Now we are being put to the test. The purpose of this book is to challenge teachers and administrators to do the following:

- Acknowledge that many theories we learned in the past must be reexamined because of the demographics of today's immigration data.
- No longer focus on the experience of mainstream Americans and

ignore the experiences, cultures, and histories of recent immigrants.

- Recognize that hosting a single annual event to demonstrate our school's concerns about its minority population is merely giving lip service to the problem; confronting bias must permeate the school calendar.
- Search out more sources of knowledge to educate ourselves about all ethnic groups and their famous citizens to effectively teach immigrant populations.
- View non-English-speaking children as a challenge not as a burden; the success we've had with our special education population should serve as a model for us.
- Be certain that plays, clubs, and teams are integrated to help children make friends with all of their classmates.
- Recognize that many immigrants believe that teachers and authority figures should not be questioned. Thus staff members must reach out to the parents of these children.
- When scheduling children, do not isolate the immigrant population in segregated classes for the entire day.
- Begin to challenge formerly accepted adages, such as "Sticks and stones will hurt my bones, but names will never harm me"; names do hurt and sometimes more than physical wounds!
- Model acceptance and respect for all children.
- Confront displays of ethnic humor since these "jokes" perpetuate stereotypes.
- Encourage staff to have high expectations for all students.
- Ensure that texts, library books, and other learning materials reflect our mission to free our school of material that stereotypes people or encourages biased assumptions.
- Confront ethnocentrism, which is the belief that one's own cultural ways are the only valid ones and are superior to all others. These attitudes existed among Germans and Japanese in World War II; recall the negative affects this thinking had on other people and nations.

There was much we had learned, but more important was our realization that we had to develop an action agenda. We wanted to survey the literature and poll our colleagues about programs they had implemented to reduce prejudice and to make parents and children feel that they were truly a part of the school and society.

Our research was extensive and the suggestions made by our staff are contained in the following list. Our challenge would be to integrate many of these activities during the school year and to put into practice the ideals we listed previously.

PROPOSED PROGRAMS AND RECOMMENDATIONS

1. Request that our school district hire a community liaison for our Hispanic community.
2. Review the board-of-education policy book and add multicultural goals to our mandates.
3. Develop a Welcome Wagon–type service to serve new residents.
4. Enlist the aid of our community service organizations in sponsoring programs.
5. Evaluate diversity programs and adopt one for use in our schools.
6. Form a multicultural club to help less fortunate community members.
7. Host an international day or an international food dinner.
8. Conduct an international olympic event as a culminating school activity.
9. Dedicate one or more bulletin boards for multiethnic news and events.
10. Hold debates and essay contests with a multiethnic focus.
11. Elicit pen pals from foreign countries for all students.
12. Have students write to travel agents and foreign consulates for brochures and materials.
13. Continue our schoolwide planning committee to evaluate our efforts.
14. Develop new in-service courses for faculty.
15. Develop a room or part of the library dedicated to an appreciation of the culture of all people.
16. Review all textbooks to eliminate those that have biased materials.
17. Develop a section of the principal's weekly memorandum to staff to contain pertinent quotes and material.

18. Write articles about our efforts to local newspapers and district newsletters.
19. Involve the PTA in sponsoring events.
20. Discuss other minority cultures that may not be represented in our school's student body.
21. Hold a student-made video festival on appreciating diversity.

The preceding proposals, described in this book, are gifts from caring teachers and principals. In our attempt to address the needs of our Hispanic children and parents, we believe similar strategies will also be useful in helping all immigrants, African Americans, and Native Americans. Principals should never foreclose on the future of any ethnic group. That's why we believe that educators are today's miracle workers.

This epilogue is a further attempt to jolt our principals into an action mode. Caring administrators, who are truly leaders of leaders, should be eager to motivate their staff members to consider several of the items in our recommendations. We are convinced that once a school's faculty is involved, they will augment our ideas and create original plans that have a more realistic chance of succeeding in their community. *Caring* is an action word, and we're confident that our nation's principals will not only accept the challenge but develop the model programs that will allow all citizens to truly become part of our schools and reap the benefits of full participation in the American dream.

References

Anti-Defamation League. (2005). *Prejudice: 101 Ways You Can Beat It.* New York: Anti-Defamation League. Reprinted with permission. All rights reserved.

Association of Teacher Educators. (1992). *African Origins.* Washington, DC: Association of Teacher Educators.

Banks, J. A., Cortés, C. E., Gay, G., Garcia, R. L., and Ochoa, A. (1991). *Curriculum Guidelines for Multicultural Education.* Washington, DC: National Council for the Social Studies. Reprinted by permission.

Lake, Robert. (1990). "An Indian Father's Plea." *Teacher's Magazine* 2(1): 48–53.

National Conference of States Legislatures. (n.d.). Immigrant Policy and Demographics. Retrieved August 5, 2005, from http://www.ncsl.org/pro grams/immig/Demographics2000Census.htm

Index

About the Authors

Robert Ricken served as principal and superintendent in the Mineola School District for 22 years and was interim superintendent in the following districts: North Bellmore, Elmont, Bellmore, Smithtown, Bellmore-Merrick, and Half Hollow Hills. He is presently teaching educational administration at Long Island University, C. W. Post. He is the author of *Love Me When I'm Most Unlovable, Book Two: The Kid's View*, *RA Guide to Nassau County Schools* (1995), *The Middle School Principal's Calendar* (1996), *The High School Principal's Calendar: A Month-by-Month Planner for the School Year* (2000), *The Elementary School Principal's Guide* (2001), and *The Middle School Principal's Calendar* (2004). He has also written articles for the *New York Times*, *Newsday*, *Sports Illustrated*, *The Harvard Review*, *Harper's Weekly*, *Read Magazine*, and *Single Parent Magazine*. He is a frequent contributor to many professional journals and has written on education for a local newspaper, *Educational Times of Long Island*.

Ricken has presented many workshops and has been the keynote speaker for the National Association of Secondary School Principals (NASSP) in New Orleans and the National Association of Middle Schools in West Virginia, Baltimore, Denver, Washington, DC, and Atlanta. He has also spoken at the National School Boards Association conference in San Francisco and Rochester and for Phi Delta Kappa at Hofstra, C. W. Post, and Molloy College. In his capacity as the Long Island coordinator of the Anti-Defamation League's A World of Difference Institute, he has conducted antibias workshops in more than 100 school districts. Locally, he has served as chairman of the board of the Nassau County Budget Committee for 4 years; board officer of School Business Partnerships of Long Island; vice president of the Nassau

County School Superintendents Association; president of Phi Delta Kappa, C. W. Post chapter; and president of the Mineola Youth Activities Committee. His awards include administrator of the year by Phi Delta Kappa, Hofstra University; administrator of the year by the Nassau-Suffolk Educator's Association; award of excellence by the National Public Relations Association; outstanding service award by the Girl Scouts of Nassau County; the Martin Luther King Jr. Recognition Award by Nassau County; and the New York State Middle School Association's Ross Burkhardt Award for Outstanding Contribution to Middle Level Education.

Michael Terc received his B.A. in mathematics and his M.A. from Hofstra University and was awarded a professional diploma in educational administration from Long Island University, C. W. Post campus. He served as an administrator in the Mineola Public School District. For 16 years, he served as assistant principal at Mineola High School, New York. Before that, he taught mathematics at Mineola Middle School for 16 years. He also served as principal of the Mineola Summer School Program for 2 years. During his career, he coached many sports and was involved in a host of student activities. He served as president of the Nassau County Baseball Coaches Association and in 1976 was selected as the *Daily News'* high school baseball coach of the year. In 1982 he authored "Coordinate Geometry and Art: A Match," published in *National Council of Mathematics Teachers Journal*. In 1994 he received the Jenkins Service Award, the highest service award given by the Mineola School District's PTA. He recently was selected by the School Administrators Association of New York State to receive its 1999–2000 New York State Distinguished Assistant Principal of the Year Award. His is author of *The Middle School Principal's Calendar: A Month-by-Month Planner for the School Year*.